Living IN THE *Power* OF THE *Spirit*

Acts 1—12

Living IN THE Power OF THE Spirit

Acts 1—12

VALERIE WILSON

Regular Baptist Press
Building Lives by the Book
www.RegularBaptistPress.org

Dedication

To Pastor Bryan Augsburger, whose love for and dedication to the Biblical text have been a source of instruction and encouragement to me, and to Jeanie Augsburger, whose eagerness to study the Word has been a blessing to me as a Bible study leader.

Other Books in This Series

Serving in the Power of the Spirit (Acts 13—20)—RBP5126
Persevering in the Power of the Spirit (Acts 21—28)—RBP5453

Living in the Power of the Spirit
© 2012 Regular Baptist Press • Schaumburg, Illinois
www.RegularBaptistPress.org • 1-800-727-4440
Printed in U.S.A. All rights reserved.
RBP5120 • ISBN: 978-1-60776-630-8

2nd printing—2014

Contents

Preface

Several years ago I had the privilege of leading the ladies of First Baptist Church in Arlington Heights, Illinois, in a study of the Gospel of John. As we neared the end of John and pondered what to study next, the ladies encouraged me to consider Acts. That seemed to make sense since Acts is really a continuation of the gospel story. For the next nine months we dedicated ourselves to an in-depth study of Acts—and that study is the basis of this guide.

The purpose of this study is to help you uncover for yourself the rich truths in this book. Each lesson is divided into two major sections: Study the Scripture and Apply the Scripture. In Study the Scripture, I will provide some historical and theological perspective from time to time, but you will need to use your Bible to discover the answers to the questions. In Apply the Scripture, I will direct your thoughts to ways you can apply the Scripture to yourself. My suggestions are only starting points. The Holy Spirit will make the truth personal to you as you depend on Him.

In teaching the ladies at First Baptist, I was able to give them resources to supplement their study. Regular Baptist Press has chosen to make these resources available to you via its website. Please read carefully "Resources for Your Study" (pp. 9, 10) before you begin this study.

Living in the power of the Spirit is an exciting life! The believers in the early church certainly knew this—and you and I can know it too! The Spirit's ministry was not limited to New Testament times. I pray that as you study Acts you will realize more of the Spirit's power in your own life.

Resources for Your Study

A number of extra resources will enhance your study of Acts 1—12. Go to www.rbpstore.org/downloads. Locate the downloads for this study, *Living in the Power of the Spirit.* The folder contains seven documents. For individual study, you will need to print *thirteen* copies of resource 1 and one copy of the remaining six resources.

 Resource 1: The Acts Acrostic will help you focus your Bible reading and study. I suggest that you read the entire Scripture passage for each lesson at one sitting. As you read, look in the text for **A**ctions of the Holy Spirit, **C**hurch Facts, **T**ransitional Details, and **S**upernatural Events. Jot down your findings on the acrostic for that lesson. Your acrostic may be slightly different from someone else's; that's okay. Some overlap between the letters is to be expected. After you have read the entire Biblical text and filled in the acrostic, go back and read the separate sections of verses, and answer the questions.

 In each lesson you will find this designation, alerting you to specific things to record on your acrostic if you have not already done so.

 Resource 2: You will use the map of New Testament Israel and the surrounding area several times during your study. Your study is enriched if you get some sense of the location of Bible places.

Resource 3: Lesson 2 includes the study of Pentecost, which often raises questions about the ministry of the Holy Spirit. This resource will help you better understand how the Spirit worked in the Old Testament and how He works now. You can check your answers in the answers section of this study guide.

Resource 4: In Acts 3 we learn of the power of Jesus' name. "Join All the Glorious Names" will help you appreciate and worship our Savior.

Resource 5: A number of Jewish religious groups are mentioned in Acts. This resource will help you understand the distinctives of these groups.

Resource 6: Stephen outlined much of Old Testament history in his sermon (Acts 7). You will be able to follow the flow of the sermon as you complete this resource.

Resource 7: Several members of the Herodian family are mentioned in Acts. Referring to this chart from time to time will help you know who's who.

God's Plan of Salvation

As you study the Scriptures—alone or with a group of women—you may realize that you have never entered into a personal relationship with Jesus Christ. We use a number of different terms to designate this relationship:

- being born again (John 3:3, 7);
- accepting the gift of eternal life (Romans 6:23);
- being saved (Acts 4:12);
- receiving Christ as Savior (John 1:12);
- becoming God's child (John 1:12).

These descriptive terms are synonymous. Sometimes it is easier to understand one concept more than another, but all of them are true of a person who "believeth in him"—that is, God's Son (John 3:16, 18, 36).

A person who wants to enter this personal relationship with Jesus Christ must acknowledge and believe five basic truths.

(1) *I am a sinner.* The Bible says, "For all have sinned, and come short of the glory of God" and "There is none righteous, no, not one" (Romans 3:23, 10). Until a person recognizes that she is a sinner in God's eyes, she will not be able to admit she needs a Savior.

(2) *God loves me.* The Bible says, "But God commendeth [showed] his love toward us, in that, while we were yet sinners, Christ died for us" (Romans 5:8). Jesus said that God loved the world of sinners so much that He sent His Son into this world (John 3:16, 17).

(3) *Jesus died for me.* The Bible says, "Who his [Jesus] own self bare our sins in his own body on the tree" and, "Forasmuch as ye know that ye were not redeemed with corruptible things, as silver and gold, . . . but with the precious blood of Christ" (1 Peter 2:24; 1:18, 19). Jesus loved *you* enough to die for *you.*

(4) *I receive Him.* The Bible says, "For the wages of sin is death; but

the gift of God is eternal life through Jesus Christ our Lord" (Romans 6:23). It also says, "For by grace are ye saved through faith; and that not of yourselves: it is the gift of God: not of works, lest any man should boast" (Ephesians 2:8, 9). The basis of our salvation is what Jesus has done for us, not what we can do for Him.

(5) *I am God's child.* The Bible says, "But as many as received him, to them gave he power to become the sons of God, even to them that believe on his name" (John 1:12). When you receive Christ by faith, God makes you His child. He is now your Heavenly Father, and this is a forever relationship! The Bible says no one or no thing can ever take you out of God's hand (John 10:28, 29), and nothing at all can ever separate you from God's love (Romans 8:38, 39).

If you are ready to make this life-changing decision, you may want to express your desire to God in prayer. "For whosoever shall call upon the name of the Lord shall be saved" (Romans 10:13). As soon as possible, tell someone else about your decision.

Welcome to God's family!

Introducing Acts

Acts 1

"But ye shall receive power, after that the Holy Ghost is come upon you: and ye shall be witnesses unto me both in Jerusalem, and in all Judaea, and in Samaria, and unto the uttermost part of the earth" (Acts 1:8).

I love books! Some of my favorite childhood memories are of trips to the library to hear the story lady. And then getting my own library card—what a thrill! I have collected books since I was a young child. While I had to cut my library rather severely when I retired, I still find it hard to resist adding new books to my library. Now I have a new way to build my library without needing any additional physical space: e-books! Even though I like to underline and write in the margins, I am finding that some books are just fine on an e-reader.

1. What are your earliest recollections of books? What are your favorite books?

When I think of books, I can't help but marvel that God chose to make the revelation of Himself "permanent" in the form of a book. He could have chosen any method of His own creating, but the Bible is a book. And this one book is actually a library all its own with sixty-six distinctive books.

The Bible is really like a continued story—especially when you read the books in chronological order. Each book builds in a unique way on the one before. In this study, you will consider the book of Acts. You undoubtedly have some knowledge of this book, even if it is limited.

2. If the Bible went from the Gospel of John to Paul's epistle to the Romans, what would we miss? What kinds of questions might we have?

Well, that is strictly a hypothetical question. We do have the book of Acts, so we are not left to wonder about these things. We will discover the answers as we study this fascinating book.

Study the Scripture

Preliminary Words (Acts 1:1–3)
Read Acts 1:1–3.

3. Do you know who the "I" is in verse 1? Are you aware of another book written to a man named Theophilus?

If you look at Luke 1:1–4, you will see that the Gospel of Luke was written by Luke to a man named Theophilus. It seems, then, that Luke was picking up in Acts where he had left off in Luke.

4. The Bible gives us some insight into the man Luke. Look at Acts 16:8–10. What do you notice about the pronouns, particularly in verse 10?

Luke may have answered the Macedonian call with Paul. We know that he sailed from Troas to Miletus with Paul (Acts 20:13). He continued on the third missionary journey with Paul (Acts 21:1), and he was with Paul on the journey to Rome (Acts 27:1).

5. What does Colossians 4:14 teach us about Luke?

The Bible does not tell us anything about Theophilus. His name means "friend of God." It is possible that he was a Roman by nationality—or at least a Gentile, as Luke was. He was either a believer already, or he was a genuine seeker, learning all he could about Christianity.

The Promise of the Holy Spirit (Acts 1:4–8)
Read Acts 1:4–8.

6. Even though the disciples had been with Jesus for forty days since the Resurrection, they still did not get the big picture. What did they think Jesus was going to do?

7. After Jesus said He would take care of kingdom details in His own time, what did He say would happen?

Acts 1:8 is the key verse for the book of Acts as well as for chapter 1. In a real sense, the verse is an outline of the book of Acts. Chapters 1—7 chronicle the work of the Spirit in Jerusalem; chapters 8—12, His work in Judea and Samaria; and chapters 13—28, "the uttermost part of the earth."

The word "witness" is an important word in Acts. As a noun or a verb, it is used twenty-nine times in the book. (You might want to make a list of the places "witness" is used as you read through the book of Acts during this study.) Our English word "martyr" is from the Greek word translated "witness."

8. How would you define what a witness is or does?

Soul-winning seems to be a spiritual gift that God gives to some people. (See, for instance, Ephesians 4:11, where the gift of evangelist is listed.) We recognize that some people do seem to have a special ability to present the gospel to people and to call for a response. Not all of us fit into this category. But we cannot excuse ourselves altogether.

Acts 1:8 makes it clear that all of us are to be *witnesses*; we are to tell others what we ourselves have experienced in our relationship with Jesus Christ.

9. What kinds of opportunities come up in everyday life to either *be* a witness or *give* a witness (or testimony)?

The Ascension (Acts 1:9–11)
Read Acts 1:9–11.

Even though Luke had told Theophilus about the Ascension at the end of the Gospel (Luke 24:50–53), it was necessary for Luke to include the details again.

10. Read John 16:7. Why did Jesus need to return to Heaven?

11. Describe what happened as the disciples watched.

 *Be sure to record a **Supernatural Event** on your Acts Acrostic: the ascension of Christ.*

The Prayer Meeting (Acts 1:12–14)
Read Acts 1:12–14.

Jesus had told the disciples to stay in Jerusalem until the Holy Spirit came (Luke 24:49), and they obeyed!

12. Where did they meet, and who was there besides the eleven disciples?

We will find the little expression "with one accord" or "in one accord" several times in the early chapters of Acts. These believers were a united group, and in this instance they were "with one accord" in prayer.

The Choice of Matthias (Acts 1:15–26)
Read Acts 1:15–26.

The disciples faced a dilemma. Judas Iscariot was no longer with them. They wanted to choose someone to fill his place so the "team" would be full strength again.

13. What were the requirements for an apostle according to verses 21 and 22?

Two men in the group met the requirements: Joseph (also called Barsabas, or Justus) and Matthias.

14. How did the group make the choice?

We understand the praying part of the process; we do that today. But what about casting lots? This practice was common in Old Testament times. When Joshua apportioned the land of Canaan to the tribes, the Bible says that he did it "by lot" (Joshua 13:6; 15:1; 16:1; 17:1; et al). We don't know exactly what this process entailed, except that God, in His sovereignty, used it to make known His will to His people. The eleven disciples used this "approved" method for picking Judas's successor.

But keep in mind that Acts is a transitional book. It bridges the gap, as it were, between the practices of God's people under the Mosaic law and the new era of the church and grace. We learn from Acts, but we do not follow all of the procedures of Acts.

 Record the Transitional Detail on your Acts Acrostic: casting lots to choose Matthias.

Apply the Scripture

- You cannot apply the Scripture if you do not know the Scripture. Take time right now to commit, before the Lord, to study each lesson carefully. Record specific items on your Acts Acrostic as you read the Scripture passage. Carefully answer the questions. Note any questions that arise in your mind as you study; ask your Bible study leader or pastor to help you find the answers.

- Look for opportunities this week to be a witness; that is, to relate to someone else what you have experienced as a child of God. Look for openings in everyday conversation with friends and family as well as people you meet in carrying out the routines of daily life.

The Beginning of the Church

Acts 2

"Then they that gladly received his word were baptized: and the same day there were added unto them about three thousand souls" *(Acts 2:41).*

In our multinational communities and with the ease of global air travel, we commonly hear other languages spoken in stores, malls, and restaurants. I regret not learning a conversational language. I studied Latin for several years—a good background for vocabulary; but I can't converse with my Hispanic neighbors.

One of the greatest linguists ever was Giuseppe Caspar Mezzofanti, who lived from 1774 to 1849. He spoke 50 languages, 39 of them fluently. In addition, he understood 57 other languages. In all, he could speak, understand, or translate 186 languages and dialects. And one more amazing fact: he never traveled outside of Italy!

Languages are important in the Biblical text for this lesson.

Study the Scripture

The Holy Spirit Comes (Acts 2:1–13)

The prefix "penta" always has something to do with the number 5. The Pentagon is a five-sided building. A pentathlon is an athletic contest with five different events.

1. Look at Leviticus 23, which describes the Jewish feasts.
  (a) What feast was celebrated on the fourteenth day of the first month?

(b)   Which feast followed on the fifteenth day?

(c)   What occurred fifty days later (v. 16)?

These feasts are the background for Acts 2. Jesus was crucified during Passover. Fifty days later Jesus' followers were gathered in the Upper Room to pray. Jews from all over the known world were gathered in Jerusalem to celebrate the Feast of Firstfruits. Acts 2:1 uses the simple designation "the day of Pentecost" to mark the date of the events that follow. Today we use the term "Pentecost" to denote the events of Acts 2. As such, Pentecost was a once-for-all event that will never be repeated.

Read Acts 2:1–4.

2. What three signs accompanied the coming of the Spirit?

-

-

-

The work and ministry of the Holy Spirit may be one of the least understood doctrines of Scripture. Because the Spirit's work is so prominent in Acts, you may want to take time to review or enhance your understanding of this important doctrine. Download resource 3, "The Ministry of the Holy Spirit" (see page 9), and complete the worksheet.

Read Acts 2:5–13.

One of the most misunderstood events of the Day of Pentecost is the event described in Acts 2:5–13: the disciples' ability to speak in other languages, sometimes called "tongues."

The Greek word translated "language" in verse 6 and "tongue" in verse 8 is the word *dialektos.* You can see the word "dialect" in that

Greek word. The word refers to a specific language of a country or district.

Unlike what sometimes occurs in religious groups today, the disciples did not pray for this supernatural event to occur. It was a direct result of the coming of the Holy Spirit.

The ability to speak in these known languages of the Jews who had gathered for Pentecost was a sign to Israel to authenticate the apostles' work. It is not an ability the Spirit gives today (even though many missionaries probably wish it were!). When the revelation of God was complete (the Scriptures), tongues ceased. (See 1 Corinthians 13:8.)

 *Record speaking in tongues as a **Transitional Detail** on your Acts Acrostic.*

Peter Preaches (Acts 2:14–40)
Read Acts 2:14–40.
3. As you read this Scripture portion, identify three main themes in Peter's message.

•

•

•

John MacArthur has noted that many churches today emphasize programs and performance. But the book of Acts puts the emphasis on preaching. "The first event of church history, following the coming of the Spirit, was Peter's sermon. . . . The book of Acts is largely the record of apostolic preaching. Preaching has always remained central to the church's mission."[1]

Read verse 38 again. Peter told the people to repent. Repentance is a change of mind and purpose that turns an individual from sin to God. Sometimes repentance is downplayed as a part of salvation. The Bible does not describe exactly what repentance "looks like," and for good reason. It may vary from person to person. But it *is* necessary. Until a person recognizes that her sin is a grievous affront to a holy God, she will not realize how desperately she needs a Savior.

If you have not come to this place in your life, you need to "listen" with your heart to Peter's sermon. Make this the day when you accept God's Son as your Savior. The plan of salvation is outlined for you on pages 11 and 12.

Acts 2:38 seems to indicate that baptism is necessary for salvation. The word "for" in the phrase "be baptized . . . for the remission of sins" can be translated "on account of" or "on the basis of." A correct translation of the phrase could be, "Be baptized on the basis of the remission [forgiveness] of your sins." The New Testament pattern is always the same: baptism follows salvation as an act of obedience. Baptism does nothing to secure a person's salvation.

The Church Begins (Acts 2:41–47)
Read Acts 2:41–47.

The church began on the Day of Pentecost. The church is not a spiritual manifestation of Old Testament Israel. Nor did it begin with Jesus and the disciples. The word "church" is not mentioned in either of those settings. (In Matthew 16:18 "church" refers to the future church, not to Israel or the disciples. In Matthew 18:17 "church" means "assembly" and, in that context, refers to the Jewish assembly.)

4. Read Ephesians 1:22 and 23 and Colossians 1:24. In these passages, what did Paul call the church?

 *Record the start of the church under **Church Facts** on your Acts Acrostic.*

The church could not begin until the Holy Spirit came and baptized believers into Christ's Body.

The church exists in two basic forms. It is *universal* in its nature: all believers in all places from Pentecost until the Rapture occurs. (See, for instance, Ephesians 1:22, 23; 5:23–29; Colossians 1:18.) The church is also *local* in nature. It is groups of believers meeting together in a given locality. (See, for instance, Acts 14:23; Romans 16:1; 1 Corinthians 1:2; Philippians 4:15.)

5. Since the early believers had no building in which to meet, what does that tell you about the meaning of the word "church"?

The final verses of Acts 2 help us understand the three main functions of a church.

6. The first function is instruction. What words in verse 42 indicate instruction?

Too often a church is judged by how many programs it has. We would do better to judge a church by how well it instructs the people of all ages who are part of that local body.

7. What opportunities for instruction does your church provide?

8. Read verses 42 and 44 again. What other function of a church do you note in these verses?

The word translated "fellowship" is the Greek word *koinonia*. It has the idea of sharing together based on our relationship to Christ.

9. What opportunities for fellowship does your church provide?

The third function of the church is worship. The people in that first church prayed together, praised together, and shared the Lord's Supper together. They were living in the power of the Spirit!

10. What opportunities for worship does your church provide?

11. What happens when a church fulfills the New Testament functions of a church? (Note verses 46 and 47.)

Apply the Scripture

- Review your answers to questions 7, 9, and 10. How well does your church measure up to the New Testament model? Is it weak in some areas and strong in others? Do you enthusiastically participate in each of the functions of your church?
- The greatest group to be part of on this earth—other than your family—is the church. Spend some time in prayer right now. Thank God for your pastor. Thank Him for the friends you have at church. Ask God to make you a productive member of His church.

Note

1. John MacArthur, *Acts: The Spread of the Gospel* (Nashville: Thomas Nelson, 2007), 11.

The Power of the Name

Acts 3

*"Then Peter said, Silver and gold have I none; but such as I have give
I thee: In the name of Jesus Christ of Nazareth rise up and walk"
(Acts 3:6).*

Names are important. They identify who we are. Have you ever looked
up the meaning of your name? If you haven't, you can probably find
the meaning on a baby names website. Do you know why your parents chose your name? Is your name the same as someone else's in the
family?

Parents pick names for their children for any number of reasons—
some of which are probably more valid than others. But seldom do
parents give the thought to naming children that Bible parents did.
Furthermore, names today do not have the same prophetic meanings
as many Bible names did.

One particular name is important in this study. It is the name
"which is above every name" and the name before which "every knee
should bow" in a day yet future (Philippians 2:9, 10).

Study the Scripture

The Miracle (Acts 3:1–10)
Read Acts 3:1–3.

1. Where were Peter and John going and at what time of day?

Even though the apostles were part of the church, which had its beginning on Pentecost (Acts 2), the temple continued to have a significant place in their lives and in the lives of the other early believers. They continued to meet at specified times for worship and prayer in the temple.

The gate mentioned in Acts 3:2 may have been the Eastern Gate, which led from the court of the Gentiles into the eastern court of the temple.

2. Look in Acts 4:22 to find the age of the man whom Peter and John encountered on the temple steps.

Giving alms was part of the Jewish religious system, so this man was probably in a good spot. When people came to the temple to perform other acts of worship, they could help a crippled beggar at the same time.

Read Acts 3:4–7.

3. Briefly describe what happened between Peter and John and the beggar.

According to Acts 2:43, the apostles performed many miracles in the early days of the church. This miracle in Acts 3 is the first one Luke recorded for us. The miracles in Acts had three distinct purposes.

- They ushered in a new era of revelation. With the start of the church, God was working with mankind in a new way. Paul referred to it as a "mystery," which had not been known before (Colossians 1:26).
- They authenticated the messengers of the new era. When God worked miracles through the apostles, He was authenticating their ministry; they had His stamp of approval. (See 1 Corinthians 1:22; the Jews liked to have signs.)
- They called listeners' attention to the new revelation. Because of the miracle in Acts 3, Peter had a platform from which to preach the gospel. As a result, thousands were added to the church (Acts 4:4).

Record this miracle as a Supernatural Event on your Acts Acrostic.

A single detail in verse 4 is interesting: "Peter, fastening his eyes upon him."

4. What do many of us do when we see people asking for money outside the grocery store, on a street corner, or even approaching our stopped vehicles?

Often we don't want to make direct eye contact. Otherwise, we are indicating we might have some interest in contributing—or at least in getting more information. Peter did not turn away from the man. He "fastened" his eyes on him; he looked at the beggar earnestly or steadfastly.

The miracle that you described in question 3 was accomplished "in the name of Jesus Christ of Nazareth."

In Bible times a person's name represented the person himself. The person's name meant everything that was true about the person. In a very real sense, the person and his name were one. Certainly that is true of our Lord. His name is synonymous with His person. And think what His name can accomplish!

5. Look up these Scripture references and complete the statements.

(a) 1 Corinthians 6:11; Acts 4:12. We are _____ in the name of the Lord.

(b) John 20:31. We have _____ through His name.

(c) Matthew 28:19; Acts 10:48. We are _____ in the name of the Lord.

(d) John 14:13, 14. We are instructed to _____ in the name of the Lord.

(e) Ephesians 5:20. We _____ _____ in the name of the Lord.

(f)   Psalm 124:8. Our _____ is in the name of the Lord.

(g)   Mark 9:41. We can _____ _____ in the name of the Lord.

(h)   Matthew 18:5. We are to minister to _____ _____ in the name of the Lord.

"There is strength in the name of the Lord;
There is pow'r in the name of the Lord;
There is hope in the name of the Lord;
Blessed is He who comes in the name of the Lord!"[1]

Read Acts 3:8–10.

6. What words did Dr. Luke "pile up" to underscore the complete effectiveness of this miracle?

The results for this man were quite dramatic! There was no denying that he was completely healed. We will see in the next lesson that the result for the apostles was a bit different.

The healed man attracted a crowd, so Peter, living in the power of the Spirit, took advantage of the situation to preach to the people.

The Message (Acts 3:11–26)
Read Acts 3:11 and 12.

In both Acts 2 and Acts 3 Peter had to correct a misunderstanding before he could start his message.

7. What was the misunderstanding in Acts 2:15?

8. What was the misunderstanding in Acts 3:12?

Read Acts 3:13–17.

Peter found an easy way to segue to the subject of Jesus, the Messiah. He picked up on familiar themes:

- Jesus came from the lineage of the patriarchs.
- Jesus was killed, but He was raised from the dead.
- You people are responsible—even though you did this in ignorance of Who Jesus truly is.

Read Acts 3:18–26.

Peter's Jewish audience was familiar with the Old Testament, so Peter used a number of references to Old Testament prophets to make his point.

9. Peter said the prophets prophesied of Christ's suffering. Name a major Old Testament prophet who foretold Christ's suffering.

10. Peter referred to Moses' words concerning Christ. If your Bible has cross-references, write the passage Peter quoted in verses 22 and 23.

11. To what prophets did Peter refer in verse 24?

Peter was making a point: You people should know about Jesus' death and resurrection because all the prophets told about it. Furthermore, Peter said, you are children of the prophets and the children of the covenant (v. 25). Peter's listeners could not excuse their ignorance.

12. Look back through Peter's entire sermon (vv. 13–26) and underline in your Bible the names he used for Jesus. (In some versions the names are easy to spot because they are capitalized.) You may choose to list the names here instead of, or in addition to, underlining them.

These were names the Jews would have recognized from the Old Testament. The Jews who witnessed this miracle should not have been at all surprised at what the apostles accomplished in the name of the Lord!

Apply the Scripture

- Look up the hymn "Join All the Glorious Names" in a hymnbook (or print resource 4). Read all five stanzas thoughtfully and prayerfully. At this point in your life's journey, which name means the most to you? Why?

- Review the statements in question 5. Thank God for what He has provided for you in Jesus' name. "O the precious name of Jesus! How it thrills our souls with joy, When His loving arms receive us And His songs our tongues employ! Precious name, O how sweet! Hope of earth and joy of heav'n; Precious name, O how sweet! Hope of earth and joy of heav'n."[2]

- Watch your speech. It is not uncommon to hear believers use expressions like "Lordy," "my Lord," "O Lord." The name of our Savior is much too precious to be used as a swear word, whether intentionally or unintentionally.

Notes

1.   Phil McHugh, Gloria Gaither, and Sandi Patty, "In the Name of the Lord" (© 1986 by River Oaks Music Co./Gaither Music Co./Sandi's Song Music).

2.   Lydia Baxter, "Take the Name of Jesus with You."

Persecution and Prayer

Acts 4:1–31

"Neither is there salvation in any other: for there is none other name under heaven given among men, whereby we must be saved" (Acts 4:12).

Do you have a prayer list? What kinds of things—or what people—are on your list? Do you pray regularly for these items and people?

Prayer is an important activity in the book of Acts. As you study this lesson, you will have an opportunity to see how your prayer requests measure up to the kind of requests made by the early Christians.

Study the Scripture

The Arrest (Acts 4:1–4)
Read Acts 4:1–4.

This passage introduces us to some of the prominent Jewish religious groups in Acts. Download resource 5, "Jewish Religious Groups in Acts," and familiarize yourself with the basic composition and beliefs of the groups you will encounter as you continue your study.

Acts 4:1 is a description of the Jewish Sanhedrin. The "captain of the temple" was second in leadership to the high priest.

1. What did the Sanhedrin do, and when did they do it (v. 3)?

The Sanhedrin had made a rule not to conduct trials after sundown. They abode by their rule in the case of Peter and John, but they certainly violated their own rule when they "tried" the Lord Jesus. (See Matthew 26:34, 57–59.)

2. According to Acts 4:4, how many men were Christ-followers by this
   time?

Counting the women, the total number was probably closer to ten
thousand. Some scholars put the number at twenty-five thousand.
With the Lord adding "to the church daily such as should be saved"
(Acts 2:47), the church grew quickly.

 *Add the size of the church to **Church Facts** (or **Supernatural**
Events) on your Acts Acrostic.*

The Address (Acts 4:5–12)
Read Acts 4:5–12.

"Name" is mentioned in verses 7, 10, and 12. You will recall from lesson 3 that the name of a person represented the person himself. The
early believers came to be known as "people of the name," the name of
Jesus Christ.

Verse 12 is one of the key salvation verses in the New Testament. If
you have not memorized this verse, please take time to do so as you
study this lesson.

3. Why is the truth of Acts 4:12 not politically correct in our day?

Peter made an interesting play on words in his address. The word
translated "made whole" in verse 9 and the word translated "saved" in
verse 12 are the same Greek word. The word means "to rescue from
danger or destruction." Peter used the word to describe both a physical
deliverance (the crippled man from his disease) and a spiritual deliverance (the believer from condemnation).

The Threat (Acts 4:13–22)
Read Acts 4:13–22.

4. What did the Jewish elders and rulers think of Peter and John
   according to verse 13?

The description does not mean they were illiterate or dumb. Rather, it means the men were uneducated in the sense of studying with a learned man and untrained in the way of the men who were questioning them. They had not been trained in rabbinic schools. The Sanhedrin did not realize that in being with Jesus, the men were both educated and trained!

5. What dilemma did the Sanhedrin face?

If you are underlining the uses of "the name" in your Bible, you will find two more references in verses 17 and 18.

6. What punishment did the Sanhedrin deliver to Peter and John?

7. How did Peter answer the Sanhedrin?

We talked in lesson 1 about the meaning of the word "witness." Verse 20 is a good description of a witness: one who speaks "the things which we have seen and heard." It's as though Peter was saying to the Sanhedrin, "We are only talking about the things we experienced ourselves."

8. When is it right to defy a government decree?

9. Recall some other Bible characters who had to defy human government.

The time may come when we will find it necessary to disobey human government in order to obey God. But even in disobedience, our attitude should be to "honour the king" (1 Peter 2:17).

The Prayer (Acts 4:23–30)
Read Acts 4:23–30.

The apostles' prayer recorded in verses 24–30 has several character-istics that should be true of our prayers as well.

- The prayer included Scripture.

10. Look at verses 25 and 26 in a study Bible. What Old Testament Scripture was quoted in the prayer?

Many of the psalms were written as prayers. If you are not in the habit of praying Scripture, the psalms are a good place to start. For example, consider Psalm 37. Praying the psalm might sound something like this: "God, please help me not to fret over people who do evil. Help me not to be jealous of the gain they have in their lives. Help me realize that evil people will soon be cut down as grass."

11. Write out your own prayer based on Psalm 37:3–7.

- The prayer did not include a request for a change in their circumstances.

If I had been praying with the apostles that day, I am sure I would have asked God to change the hearts of the Sanhedrin and make those men amenable to the gospel message. But you won't find that kind of request in this prayer. The apostles did not ask for protection; they prayed for power. "They did not pray to have their circumstances changed or their enemies out of office. Rather, they asked God to empower them to make the best use of their circumstances."[1]

- The prayer acknowledged God's sovereignty.

God's sovereignty means He is in control; He is the supreme ruler. "He does whatever pleases Him and determines whether we can do what we have planned. This is the essence of God's sovereignty; His absolute independence to do as He pleases and His absolute control over the actions of all His creatures. No creature, person, or empire can either thwart His will or act outside the bounds of His will."[2]

12. What words in the prayer refer to God's sovereignty?

The early believers affirmed God's sovereignty; He was the ruler over all, and His will would be done. But that did not take away their human responsibility.

13. What did they pray for (v. 29)?

Augustine said, "Pray as though everything depends on God, and work as though everything depends on you."

 *Verse 30 includes a **Transitional Detail**: praying for the power to do signs and wonders. Record this detail on your Acts Acrostic.*

The Results (Acts 4:31)
Read Acts 4:31.

Verse 31 does not describe a second Pentecost. The verse speaks of the filling of the Spirit. Ephesians 5:18 provides clear teaching on the filling of the Spirit. Our English Bibles read, "Be filled with the Spirit"; but the Greek verb tense indicates continuous action; so the words could accurately be translated, "Keep on being filled." Filling is a repeated ministry of the Spirit. We have all of the Spirit we will ever have; He indwells us. The filling of the Spirit concerns letting the Spirit have all of us. It describes living life in the power of the Spirit.

Record the filling of the Spirit as an Action of the Holy Spirit on your Acts Acrostic.

Apply the Scripture

- How do your prayers measure up to the prayers of the early believers? When you thought about your prayer list at the beginning of this lesson, did you include boldness to witness or an acknowledging of God's sovereignty? So often our requests center on temporal, or physical, needs. Such requests are not wrong, but our prayers need to be broader than that. Ask God to help you make some changes in your prayer life. Start to use Scripture in your prayers; accept your circumstances rather than praying for them to change; acknowledge God's sovereignty.

- It is possible that persecution of true believers is closer than we think. If we expect to be bold in persecution, we need to start now. We need boldness to share Christ in our homes, workplaces, communities. Add the prayer request of Acts 4:29 to your personal prayer list.

Notes
1. Warren Wiersbe, *Be Dynamic* (Wheaton, IL: Victor Books, 1987), 54.
2. Jerry Bridges, *Trusting God Even When Life Hurts* (Colorado Springs: NavPress, 1988), 36.

Tell the Truth!

Acts 4:32—5:11

"And the multitude of them that believed were of one heart and of one soul: neither said any of them that ought of the things which he possessed was his own; but they had all things common" (Acts 4:32).

A graduate of LeTourneau University in Longview, Texas, test-drives big equipment for the John Deere Company. His college nickname was "Sugar." He got the nickname because of his energetic behavior, which his dorm mates described as being on a "sugar high." The young man said the name might not have stuck, "except I would turn beet red every time the girls on our sister floor would say, 'Hey, Sugar.'"

Do you have a nickname? How did you acquire the nickname?

Today's lesson contains the account of a man who lived up to his nickname.

Study the Scripture

Sharing (Acts 4:32–37)
Read Acts 4:32–35.
   1. What was a common practice in the early church?

Some people have used this passage to support the idea of communism: from each according to his ability; to each according to his need. But that is a misuse of the passage for several reasons.

• The Jewish believers, who made up the majority of the early church, were familiar with the Old Testament Scriptures.

2. Read Leviticus 19:10; 23:22; Deuteronomy 15:7–11. What is the main teaching in these verses?

- Slavery was common in New Testament times, and converted slaves were part of the church. In addition, some people may have lost their jobs when they trusted Christ. So the church would have included many needy people.
- This sharing of goods was a voluntary practice. Nowhere do we read a command to the church to do this.
- Not everybody participated in the practice.

3. Look at Acts 4:35 again. To whom was the distribution made?

This practice was not an attempt to equalize the wealth among all the people.

   • The practice is not mentioned in any of the Epistles; it did not continue as the church progressed. It was a transitional practice.

 *Note sharing of goods as a **Transitional Detail** on your Acts Acrostic.*

Read Acts 4:36 and 37.

4. These verses introduce us to Barnabas. What facts do you learn about him in these two verses?
    •

    •

    •

    •

    •

    •

-

-

You may remember that the Levites did not own property in Old Testament times (Numbers 18:20, 24). Several times in Joshua we read that the Levites did not have an inheritance because the Lord was their inheritance (Joshua 13:33; 18:7; et al.). While the Levites did not own land in Israel, it may have been permissible by New Testament times to own land outside of Israel.

Sinning (Acts 5:1–11)

We learned in Acts 3 and 4 that Satan attempted to disrupt the work of the apostles by means of persecution. Nevertheless, the church continued to grow. But Satan is ever the enemy of God's people and God's work. We must never underestimate his craftiness! He tried a new tactic as we will see in Acts 5.

Read Acts 5:1–11.

5. According to verses 1 and 2, what did Ananias and Sapphira do?

Before we study what went wrong, keep two things in mind: (1) Ananias and Sapphira did not have to sell their land; they were not commanded to do so; (2) if they did choose to sell the land, they were not obligated to give all the proceeds of the sale.

So where did Ananias and Sapphira go wrong?

6. What sin is mentioned in verse 3?

7. What sin is mentioned in verse 9?

"To 'test the Holy Spirit' is to see how much one can get away with before He judges; it means to presume on Him, to see if He will perform His Word, or to stretch Him to the limits of judgment."[1]

A third sin is suggested in the text though not explicitly stated.

8. (a) What is it that makes us want to look good in other people's eyes?

(b) What would Ananias and Sapphira have wanted the apostles to think about them because they brought such a large sum of money?

The Bible repeatedly warns against this sin.

9. Summarize each of the following verses.

Romans 12:3

Proverbs 11:2

Proverbs 16:18

Proverbs 6:16, 17

1 Peter 5:5

10. How were Ananias and Sapphira punished?

 Record the death of Ananias and Sapphira as a Supernatural Event on your Acts Acrostic.

Someone once observed that if God struck down every church member who lied today, not many members would be left.

11. Think about it: Why was the punishment so severe?

It seems that when God starts a new work—such as the birth of the church—the punishment for sin is administered swiftly.

12. Read Leviticus 10:1 and 2. God had given the law and instituted the priesthood and sacrificial system. What happened when Nadab and Abihu did things their own way?

13. Read Joshua 7:20–26. The Israelites had just entered the Promised Land, starting a new chapter in their history. What did Achan do and what happened to him?

God's view of sin does not change over time; sin will always be punished. But at the outset of a new work, God makes a strong statement concerning the blessings of obedience and the results of disobedience.

14. When all this with Ananias and Sapphira was over, what was the result in the church?

The Greek word for "fear" is *phobos*, from which we get the English word "phobia." We tend to think of phobias as trivial fears, but the Greek word actually means "dread" or "terror." I'm sure that if I had been in that first Jerusalem church, I would have experienced *phobos* as well!

We note one other interesting fact in verse 11. This is the first use of the word "church" in Acts. (Acts 2:47 is more accurately translated, "The Lord added to their number." "Church" was inserted by the translators of the King James Version.)

*Add this first use of the word "church" to **Church Facts** on your Acts Acrostic.*

Apply the Scripture

- Most likely your church does not practice the sale of property and the distribution of the proceeds to the needy in your church. But we are part of the "community of saints," so how should we meet the needs of others in our midst? List some possible ideas.

- Read Matthew 6:1–4. What is the principle in these verses? If Ananias and Sapphira had been less interested in man's acclaim and more concerned about God's approval, they might have had longer lives! When you have an opportunity to share some of your resources for the benefits of others, remember the secrecy principle!

Note

1.   John Walvoord and Roy Zuck, eds., *The Bible Knowledge Commentary: New Testament* (Wheaton, IL: Victor Books, 1983), 365.

Choosing to Obey God

Acts 5:12–42

"Then Peter and the other apostles answered and said, We ought to obey God rather than men" (Acts 5:29).

Have you ever been part of something new? Maybe you have been part of a newly formed Sunday School class or even a new church. Maybe you were among the first occupants of a new building development. Maybe you've been involved in a start-up business. Think about your experience.

1. What is it like to be part of a "first"? What are some of the advantages? What about the disadvantages?

As we study Acts, we need to remember that the church was new. The people who were "added to the church" (Acts 2:47) experienced all the advantages and disadvantages of being first. This study gives us more insight into the experiences of the first church.

Study the Scripture

The Church Grows (Acts 5:12–16)
Read Acts 5:12–16.

2. Review the first eleven verses of Acts 5. What event is recorded?

Undoubtedly the members of the church were making sure their motives and actions were pleasing to God as they reflected on what happened to two of their group.

Verse 12 indicates that believers met together in Solomon's Porch. This area was a vast concourse along the east side of the temple. It was an ideal spot for meetings. (Remember that the early church did not meet in church buildings.) It was also a good place for believers to meet with questioning, interested Jews.

3. This passage mentions several Transitional Details; that is, things that did not continue beyond the early years of the church. List two or three items that you note.

4. Read Acts 4:30. How does that verse relate to Acts 5:12?

The people had prayed for the power to do signs and wonders, and God answered their prayer.

 *Add apostles did signs and wonders to the **Transitional** Details on the Acts Acrostic for lesson 6.*

Verse 14 records that "multitudes both of men and women" believed and were added to the church. God was doing a new thing, and even the rapid growth of the church was evidence that this was, indeed, God's work. Rarely in church history have "multitudes" of people genuinely believed. Living in the power of the Spirit was an exciting life!

 *Add rapid growth of the church as another **Transitional** Detail.*

5. What was unique about the healings recorded in verse 15?

*Add a final **Transitional Detail**: healing of sick and demon-possessed people.*

Remember that miracles were used to validate God's new dealing with people. Since "the Jews require a sign" (1 Corinthians 1:22), we have some idea of how convincing these miracles must have been to them.

These healings are transitional because the time for such miracles has passed. We have the complete revelation of God, the Bible. We don't need anything else. (See 1 Corinthians 13:8–10.)

6. Read John 14:26 and 1 Corinthians 2:9–13. How are we able to understand the truth of God's Word?

The Council Is Upset (Acts 5:17–32)
Read Acts 5:17 and 18.

Verse 17 reminds us of the composition of the council, or Sanhedrin. The majority of the group were Sadducees, and the high priest, the leader of the council, was a Sadducee. The other group, the Pharisees, was the minority group in the Sanhedrin.

7. List a reason or two for the council's indignation.

Once again the apostles found themselves in prison. But it wouldn't be for long. (All twelve apostles seem to have been involved here, not just one or two of them.)

Read Acts 5:19–21.

8. Describe the apostles' release.

You have to think that God has a sense of humor. Of all the ways God could have released the men from prison, He chose to do it with an angel! Do you recall from resource 5 (lesson 4) that the Sadducees did not believe in angels?

9. What did the apostles do upon their release?

You need to understand this setting: The apostles started teaching in the temple early in the morning. In another part of the temple complex, the time came for the council to meet. The members of the council wanted to hear from the apostles, so they dispatched officers to bring the prisoners to the council chambers when, in fact, the "prisoners" were almost right under their noses.

Read Acts 5:22–26.

10. What report did the officers bring back?

Another bit of humor injected by Dr. Luke, the human writer. The guards had spent the night guarding an empty cell!

11. While the officers were giving their report, another messenger came to the council. What did he report?

The captain and officers went to investigate, and the apostles willingly went with them to the council chambers. The captain was certainly relieved that the men went willingly. Christianity was popular with the people, and the captain feared for his life if he had had to make an arrest.

Read Acts 5:27 and 28.

12. Rather than obeying the orders of the Sanhedrin ("Did not we straitly command you?"), what had the apostles done (according to the high priest)?

The high priest expressed concern that the apostles were intending to "bring this man's blood upon us." To grasp his concern, you need to understand a principle from the Mosaic law. When the blood of an innocent man was shed, the guilt of his death, his blood, was "upon" the people who had allowed it to happen (Deuteronomy 19:10).

13. Read Matthew 27:25. (a) What did the crowd cry out?

(b) What were they admitting with this cry?

The high priest seemed to be afraid that the blood of an innocent Man might truly be upon him.

Read Acts 5:29–32.

Peter, living in the power of the Spirit, took every opportunity he had to present the truth about Jesus the Messiah, and this occasion was no exception. After declaring that his highest allegiance was to God, Peter spoke of the death and resurrection of Christ.

Verse 29 is the key verse for this lesson. We looked at obedience to the Highest Authority in lesson 4. God's orders were to be obeyed over those of the Sanhedrin!

The Council Is Appeased (Acts 5:33–39)
Read Acts 5:33–39.

14. How did the Sanhedrin respond to Peter's words?

In the midst of the confusion, a man named Gamaliel stood up. He is described as "a doctor of the law"; that is, he was a specialist in the writings of Moses. He was also a Pharisee, a member of the minority group in the Sanhedrin. He was respected enough that the group listened to him.

15. Summarize the argument Gamaliel made to the council.

We don't know from historical writings about the uprising caused by Theudas. Josephus, the first-century Jewish historian, mentions a man by that name, but he lived long after Acts was written. Theudas was evidently a common name.

Judas led a revolt against Rome in AD 6. He claimed it was treason to pay tribute to Caesar. The uprising was crushed by Cyrenius, the governor of Syria. (Does that name sound familiar? Read Luke 2:2 to refresh your memory.)

Bible scholars hold different views of Gamaliel. Some say he was a wise man who defused a tense situation. Others say he was a weak man because he did not urge the council to investigate the claims of Christianity; he should not have assumed it would come to naught.

The Church Leaders Are Persecuted (Acts 5:40–42)
Read Acts 5:40–42.

16. After agreeing with Gamaliel, what did the council do?

This beating was not a casual slap on the wrist. It was a flogging, which was common in New Testament times. The victim received thirty-nine stripes with a whip that had pieces of metal or glass tied to the ends. Normally two lashes were administered to the back for every one delivered to the chest. Hence the number of lashes was divisible by three. Another reason for thirty-nine lashes is found in Deuteronomy 25:3. Forty lashes were allowed, but no Jew wanted to make a mistake and exceed that number. (This was the same kind of beating our Savior endured [Matthew 27:26].)

17. How did the apostles react to this severe physical punishment?

Nothing could deter these determined apostles! They had seen the risen Christ, and their lives had been transformed.

Apply the Scripture

- What would your town, village, city look like if it were "filled" with the gospel message? What can you do to "fill" the area right around your home?
- How can a believer rejoice in suffering? Meditate on these verses on this subject: Philippians 1:29; 1 Peter 2:21; 4:12–16; John 15:18–21; 16:1–4.
- Remember to pray for believers in countries where persecution is severe; for example, China, India, North Korea, Muslim countries.

Serving in the Church

Acts 6:1—7:1

"Wherefore, brethren, look ye out among you seven men of honest report, full of the Holy Ghost and wisdom, whom we may appoint over this business" (Acts 6:3).

You may be in a large church, a small one, or one in between. Regardless of the size, your pastor probably does not do all the work of the church by himself. Your church has some elected and appointed officers. Do you know who these people are? Do you know the process by which they were elected or chosen?

The early church faced a new situation: the apostles couldn't get all the work done! The book of Acts helps us understand how the church solved that problem—and it gives us guidance for how our churches today choose or elect those who will serve.

Study the Scripture

Situation (Acts 6:1)
Read Acts 6:1.
1. What two groups of people are named in this verse?

Both of these groups were Jews, but each group had distinctive characteristics. The Hebrews were Jews who lived in Palestine and who spoke Aramaic (also called Syriac). This was the common Jewish language of that day; Jesus spoke Aramaic. These Jews also used the Hebrew Scriptures, so they were able to read, understand, and speak Hebrew.

The Hellenists, or Grecians, on the other hand, were Greek-cultured Jews. They may have been born outside Israel and then moved back. They spoke Greek. These Jews used the Greek translation of the Hebrew Old Testament, called the Septuagint.

2. Considering these characteristics, what kinds of problems might arise between the two groups?

3. What problem did arise?

4. Look at Acts 2:45 and 4:35. What was the "daily ministration" (or "distribution")?

Some people would advocate this kind of communal sharing today, but Acts makes it clear that such sharing was not without its problems. Ananias and Sapphira died because they were deceitful over the amount they contributed. And then murmuring about who was getting what threatened the unity of the church.

Solution (Acts 6:2–7)
Read Acts 6:2.

5. Who initiated the meeting described in verse 2? What was their view of the problem?

The meaning of "serve tables" in Acts is not necessarily the same idea as being a waitperson in a restaurant in our culture. The Greek word for "table" can mean a place for eating, but it can also mean a bank or a place where money is exchanged. The word is translated "bank" in Luke 19:23. In John 2:15 the word is used for the money-changers' tables. Here in Acts the word may refer to a daily distribution of food, a distribution of money, or a distribution of both.

The Greek word translated "serve" in Acts 6:2 is translated "ministry" in verse 4. Serving tables and ministering the Word were both essential ministries of the church.

The care of widows is an important concern for the church.
6. Summarize the teaching of 1 Timothy 5:3 and James 1:27.

Read Acts 6:3–7.
7. The apostles suggested that the church appoint seven men to care
   for the physical needs of the people. What three qualities were these
   men to have?

   •

   •

   •

8. Considering the problem facing the church, why were these qualities important?

All the men who were chosen had Greek names, but they were not
necessarily Hellenists (although some Bible scholars think they were).
Greek names were not uncommon. One of the men, Nicolas of Antioch,
was a Gentile; he was a proselyte to Judaism.

 Make sure to record helpers chosen for the apostles as a Church Fact on your Acts Acrostic.

Note three important words in verse 5: "And they chose." "The
whole multitude," the entire church, was together and made the decision. This is congregational church government. Baptists believe that a
local church should be autonomous. "Autonomy" means that a church
operates without outside control and that it exists independently. It is
a self-governing body, free from all ecclesiastical control.

 Also add congregational government as a Church Fact.

9. How did the apostles "certify" these men for service?

10. Think about what you know of the rest of the book of Acts. How many of these men are mentioned again in the book?

Lots of work gets done when no one cares who gets the credit. When self gets in the way, the work is compromised. The other five men evidently served very effectively even though we never read of them again.

The question arises when studying this passage: Were these seven men the first deacons? Bible scholars do not agree on an answer, as the following excerpts reveal.

"The Greek word for 'serve' is the one from which we derive 'deacon,' but these men were 'deacons' only in the sense of being servants. They were not yet deacons in the later sense of officers in the church."[1]

"Inasmuch as the epistles indicate the existence of officers called deacons who appear to be secondary to the leaders of the church . . . and since there is no other place where their ministry is described, it seems very possible that their origin should be traced to the Seven."[2]

"These seven men held a temporary position for the purpose of meeting a specific need. This seems to be the best approach. . . . Even so, these men do illustrate the role and function of the office of deacons."[3]

Perhaps the best answer to the question is simply to admit that if these men were not the first deacons, they were the forerunners of that church office.

11. What were the results after the problem was solved?

   •

   •

   •

The priests who believed were probably not the Sadducean aristocrats who were part of the Sanhedrin. As many as eight thousand temple priests may have been in Jerusalem. Many of them were godly men. Zacharias (Luke 1:5, 6) was one such priest. How exciting to think that "a great company" of these men who were involved in Israel's sacrificial system came to accept the Lamb of God as the final Sacrifice for their sins.

Stephen (Acts 6:8—7:1)
Read Acts 6:8-10.

The remainder of chapter 6 and all of chapter 7 is devoted to one of the men who had been chosen to help the apostles: Stephen.

12. How is Stephen described in verse 8?

-

-

-

Stephen's name means "crown." Two Greek words are used for "crown" in the New Testament: (1) *diadema*, which means "royal crown"; we get the English word "diadem" from the Greek word; (2) *stephanos*, which means "victor's crown"; it is the basis for the name "Stephen." Wiersbe makes the point that you can inherit a *diadema*, but you can only earn a *stephanos*.[4] Stephen lived up to his name, as we shall see in the next lesson.

Verse 9 refers to the synagogue of the libertines, or freedmen. Freedmen were former slaves. The members of this synagogue were Jewish freedmen, or descendants of freedmen, from the places listed in the verse.

We can only assume that Stephen went to this synagogue to present the gospel. Verse 10 would indicate that he was quite effective in his ministry. But the Jews were not happy!

Read Acts 6:11—7:1.

13. Of what did the Jews accuse Stephen before the Sanhedrin ("council," vv. 11–14)?

14. How did Stephen appear to the men of the council?

The high priest mentioned in Acts 7:1 is most likely Caiaphas, the same high priest when Jesus was crucified (Matthew 26:3). In the next lesson we will look carefully at Stephen's response to the council.

Apply the Scripture

- What did you learn in this lesson about the organization of the church? Does the same organization work in all situations and at all times?
- What did you learn in this lesson about serving in the church?
- Take time this week to express appreciation to people in your church who serve in ways that are largely unseen by most of the congregation; for example, the janitorial staff, nursery workers, your child's Sunday School teacher.

Notes

1.   Charles Ryrie, The Ryrie Study Bible (Chicago: Moody Press), note on Acts 6:2; 1654.

2.   Homer Kent Jr., *Jerusalem to Rome: Studies in the Book of Acts* (Grand Rapids: Baker Academic, 1972), 63.

3.   Walvoord and Zuck, 368.

4.   Wiersbe, 83.

LESSON 8

Faithful unto Death

Acts 7:2—8:4

"Therefore they that were scattered abroad went every where preaching the word" (Acts 8:4).

1. How familiar are you with Old Testament people and events? Number these fifteen names and events in chronological order.
   ___ Divided Kingdom
   ___ Moses
   ___ David
   ___ Esther
   ___ Adam
   ___ Saul
   ___ the Flood
   ___ Solomon
   ___ Abraham
   ___ Ruth
   ___ Captivity
   ___ Joshua
   ___ Joseph
   ___ Malachi
   ___ the Exodus

Stephen, one of the seven men chosen to help the apostles in the first church, had a wonderful grasp of the Old Testament, and he was able to recall the details under the most difficult of circumstances. Print resource 6 ("Stephen's Sermon before the Sanhedrin") so that you can outline Stephen's discourse as you study this Scripture passage.

Study the Scripture

Stephen's Sermon (Acts 7:2–53)
Read Acts 7:2–8.
2. Review the previous lesson. Why did Stephen appear before the
   Sanhedrin?

The Jews liked historical reviews, so Stephen's discourse would have
appealed to his listeners—at least at first. Eventually, though, Stephen
would show that the Christian message was fully consistent with Old
Testament revelation.
3. How did Stephen describe God as he started his sermon?

4. What did Stephen see at the end of the day (v. 55)?

5. List here—or on your copy of "Stephen's Sermon before the Sanhedrin" (resource 6)—six things Stephen said about Abraham.
   •

   •

   •

   •

   •

   •

Read Acts 7:8–16.
6. Verse 8 names Abraham's descendants: Isaac, Jacob, the twelve
   patriarchs (sons of Jacob). Verses 9–16 deal with one of Jacob's sons,
   Joseph. List several facts about Joseph, Jacob, and Egypt (or use
   resource 6).

-

-

-

-

-

-

-

-

Read Acts 7:17–29.

7. Verses 17–19 describe conditions in Egypt between Joseph and Moses. How would you characterize this period of time?

8. Verses 20–29 describe the first forty years of Moses' life. Record several significant events here or on resource 6.

-

-

-

-

-

-

Read Acts 7:30–35.

9. These verses describe Moses' second forty years of life. Note two significant details.

  •

  •

Read Acts 7:36–44.

10. This final section on Moses' life describes the last forty years. Write a few details. (The word "church" in verse 38 means the "assembly" of the Israelites.)

  •

  •

  •

  •

Read Acts 7:45–50.

11. What men did Stephen name as he finished his summary of Israel's history?

Read Acts 7:51–53.

12. Stephen then began to discuss the Jews' responsibility. List four things Stephen said about the Jews. (Or use resource 6.)

  •

  •

  •

  •

Stephen's Stoning (Acts 7:54–60; 8:2)
Read Acts 7:54–60 and 8:2.

The Sanhedrin became a riotous mob, and the result was mob violence. What the council did was illegal. Jewish law specified that a capital case must have a second trial at least one day later. Stoning was the punishment for blasphemy according to the Mosaic law (Leviticus 24:16), but the Romans did not allow the Sanhedrin to execute prisoners. So the Sanhedrin was in violation of its own law—and Roman law—in several ways.

13. What similarities do you see between Stephen's death and Jesus' death?

14. Read Revelation 2:10. How did Stephen live up to his name? (See page 55 to review the meaning of his name.)

15. Compare Hebrews 10:12 with Acts 7:55 and 56. What difference do you notice?

16. What does this difference suggest?

Verse 60 says that Stephen "fell asleep." The Bible uses this language to describe a believer's death. (See, for instance, John 11:11; 1 Corinthians 11:30; 1 Thessalonians 4:13.) This is not "soul sleep"; the soul is very much alive. When a believer dies, the *body* is asleep in the grave until the time of the Rapture (1 Thessalonians 4:13–16); the *soul* goes immediately to the presence of the Lord (2 Corinthians 5:6, 8).

*Record Stephen's martyrdom as a **Church Fact** on your Acts Acrostic.*

Saul's Support (Acts 8:1, 3)

Read Acts 7:58; 8:1 and 3.

This is our first introduction to Saul, who was most likely a member of the Sanhedrin. Saul became the number one persecutor of the early church. Later in his life, he would describe himself as a blasphemer, a persecutor, an injurious (insolent) man, and the chief of sinners (1 Timothy 1:13, 15). Jesus had foretold just such persecution: "The time cometh, that whosoever killeth you will think that he doeth God service" (John 16:2).

17. Why do you think Stephen's death did not placate those who were opposed to the gospel?

The Gospel's Spread (Acts 8:4)

Read Acts 8:4.

18. What was the overall result of Stephen's death?

Look at the map of Israel (resource 2). This persecution and Stephen's death catapulted the believers from Jerusalem into Judea and Samaria, thus fulfilling part of Jesus' mission for the church (Acts 1:8).

Apply the Scripture

- In January 1956 five young missionary men were martyred by Auca Indians in Ecuador. Their martyrdom launched the missionary careers of untold hundreds of young people who were determined to take the gospel around the world. Jim Elliot, one of the five, kept a journal of his spiritual journey. You may recall this quote from his journal: "He is no fool who gives what he cannot keep to gain what he cannot lose." A few months later, Jim wrote, "I must not think it strange if God takes in youth those whom I would have kept on earth till they were older. God is peopling Eternity, and I must not restrict Him to old men and women."[1]

You may know the rest of the story of the Aucas. Because missionaries persevered in taking the gospel to them, scores of Auca Indians will meet the martyrs in Heaven.

You can read more about these martyrs in books such as *Through Gates of Splendor* and *Shadow of the Almighty,* both by Elisabeth Elliot. *Beyond the Gates of Splendor* and *End of the Spear* are DVDs that chronicle the spread of the gospel among the Auca Indians.

- The history of the church is marked by the blood of martyrs. A classic book, *Fox's Book of Martyrs: A History of the Lives, Sufferings, and Deaths of the Early Christian and Protestant Martyrs* by John Foxe, is still available in print or for e-readers.

- Severe persecution, even martyrdom, is part of life for believers in many countries today. Sign up to receive e-mail updates from websites like persecution.com sponsored by The Voice of the Martyrs.

- God doesn't call all of us to be martyrs, but He does call all of us to live for Him, to present our bodies as living sacrifices (Romans 12:1). In living for Him and in the power of the Spirit, we need to be prepared to die for Him. Jesus said, "Be thou faithful unto death, and I will give thee a crown of life" (Revelation 2:10).

Note

1. Quotations from Jim Elliot's journals quoted by Elisabeth Elliot, *Shadow of the Almighty* (New York: Harper & Brothers, 1958), 108, 117.

Counterfeit and Genuine

Acts 8:5–40

"Then Philip opened his mouth, and began at the same scripture, and preached unto him Jesus" (Acts 8:35).

Counterfeit money is a big problem in our society. The government continues to work on ways to make it more and more difficult for people to make counterfeit bills. On a government website about detecting counterfeit money, the fake bill is always shown beside the real one. To detect a counterfeit, one must be a student of the real thing.

Religious "counterfeits" abound as well. There will always be people who think they can gain something by claiming to be someone they are not. Acts 8 introduces us to a man who was probably a counterfeit believer and to another man who was genuinely converted. You will be able to note the differences in the two men as you study the Scripture.

Study the Scripture

Samaria (Acts 8:5–8)
Read Acts 8:5–8.

This passage introduces us to the ministry of another of the Seven (Acts 6:5), Philip.

1. Read Acts 21:8. What is Philip called in this verse?

Samaria was a region in Israel between Galilee on the north and Judea on the south. (Check the location on the map, resource 2.) In Old Testament times Samaria was the capital of the Northern Kingdom (Israel). In 722 BC the city and the kingdom were captured by the Assyrians. The Assyrians removed some of the Hebrews; then they brought in other people to repopulate the land by intermarrying with the Hebrews (2 Kings 17:24). These mixed Jews stopped worshiping at the temple in Jerusalem and worshiped instead at Mount Gerizim. ("This mountain" in John 4:20 and 21 is Mount Gerizim.)

2. Read John 4:9. How did the Jews treat the Samaritans?

Philip was obedient to the Lord's leading and went to Samaria. But "for Philip to share his faith with the Samaritans was a most uncommon act."[1]

3. How does Philip's preaching in Samaria relate to Acts 1:8?

4. What kind of ministry did Philip have in Samaria?

Simon (Acts 8:9–25)
Read Acts 8:9–13.

5. What was Simon's background or profession?

Sorcery, a kind of magic, dated back to the Medo-Persians. It was a "mixture of science and superstition, including astrology, divination, and the occult."[2]

6. What happened when Simon encountered Philip?

Read Acts 8:14–17.

7. Why did Peter and John go to Samaria?

8. What did Peter and John do when they got to Samaria?

Record this Transitional Detail on your Acts Acrostic: Peter and John prayed for the Samaritan believers to receive the Holy Spirit.

As we continue to study the growth of the church as recorded in Acts, we must remember the transitional nature of the book. God was doing a new thing, and He validated that work in different ways. The Jews needed a strong sign that the despised Samaritans could be part of the Body of Christ. The Holy Spirit came to the Samaritans in a way similar to His coming at Pentecost, thus connecting Philip's work in Samaria with the work of the other apostles in Jerusalem.

Read Acts 8:17–25.
9. Summarize the exchange between Peter and Simon.

10. Do you think Simon was a genuine believer or a counterfeit? Support your answer.

Salvation (Acts 8:26–40)
Read Acts 8:26–30.
11. How did God redirect Philip's ministry?

Locate this area on the map (resource 2).
12. Who else was on the road and why?

Philip was an obedient servant. Verse 26 records that the Angel of the Lord told Philip to go to Gaza; verse 27 says he arose and went.

Verse 29 records the Spirit's urging Philip to go the chariot; verse 30 says Philip ran to the chariot.

13. How did Philip begin his interaction with the Ethiopian?

Read Acts 8:31–35.

14. What passage of Scripture was the Ethiopian reading?

Philip *started* at that Scripture and presented Christ to this searching soul. Undoubtedly Philip showed how the Son of God fulfilled Old Testament prophecy and also told of His death and resurrection, which Philip had perhaps witnessed firsthand.

Read Acts 8:36–39.

15. What did the Ethiopian want to do?

16. What did Philip need to know before he agreed to the man's baptism?

The English word "baptism" is from the Greek word *baptizo.* The word means "to immerse." If the Greeks had had coffee makers, the bottom of the unit would have said, "Do not *baptizo.*" In addition to the meaning of the Greek word, the words "down . . . into the water" and "come up out of the water" also indicate that Philip immersed the Ethiopian.

Technically, it is incorrect to speak of "modes of baptism." Sprinkling and pouring may be choices some churches make, but they are not ways of "immersing." There is only one way to immerse, and that is to submerge in water.

People are called "Baptists" because they believe in and practice immersion. "Baptizers" existed before the Reformation, so Baptists are not really a product of the Protestant Reformation.

Baptism does not save or provide any grace to the one baptized. Baptism is obedience to Jesus' last command (Matthew 28:19, 20).

The New Testament pattern is always belief, then baptism. (See, for instance, Acts 2:41; 10:44–48; 16:14, 15.) Baptism identifies a person as a believer and demonstrates the new life the believer now possesses (Romans 6:4).

 Add this Church Fact to your Acts Acrostic: Believer's baptism is practiced.

Read Acts 8:39 and 40.
17. What happened to Philip and the treasurer after the baptism?

 Acts 8 includes some definitive Actions of the Holy Spirit. If you have not already done so, add directed Philip to the Ethiopian and took Philip away to your Acts Acrostic.

Apply the Scripture

- Philip was willing to take the gospel to a group of people who were not in his comfort zone. What groups of people live in your neighborhood, town, or city? Some of these groups are probably outside *your* comfort zone. What do you do personally or what does your church do to give the gospel to these people?
- What Bible passages could you use to present the plan of salvation to someone else? Have you memorized these verses? If not, determine to do so over the next few weeks.
- Have you experienced believer's baptism? If you are a genuine believer, baptism is the next step in your obedience to Christ. Talk to your pastor about this important matter.

Notes
1. Kent, 78.
2. MacArthur, 38.

An Amazing Conversion

Acts 9:1–31

"But the Lord said unto him, Go thy way: for he is a chosen vessel unto me, to bear my name before the Gentiles, and kings, and the children of Israel: For I will shew him how great things he must suffer for my name's sake" (Acts 9:15, 16).

Listening to people recount how they came to faith in Christ is always an enjoyable experience. Some conversion experiences—like mine—occur in the hearts of young children who realize they are sinners and need Jesus to save them. Often children who come to faith at a young age are being reared in homes with parents who love the Lord. Some conversion experiences occur when teens or young adults respond to the gospel and leave the "religion" that is practiced—or at least professed—in their homes. The older a person is when he or she trusts the Savior, the more dramatic the conversion experience is apt to be. But written across all these experiences—from the youngest child to the oldest believer—are the words "By grace . . . through faith . . . not of works" (Ephesians 2:8, 9).

In a very real sense, every conversion experience is amazing because it is God's work to impart life to one who is dead in trespasses and sins (Ephesians 2:1). But the circumstances of some conversions are just more amazing than others; and the conversion of Saul the persecutor fits into this latter category. Let's look more closely at what happened on the road to Damascus.

Study the Scripture

Saul's Quest (Acts 9:1, 2)
Read Acts 9:1 and 2.

On the map (resource 2), locate Damascus. It was the capital of Syria and was about 150 miles from Jerusalem. It took about a week to make the journey between the two cities. Evidently many believers had fled from Jerusalem to Damascus in the persecution described in Acts 8. It's interesting to note that the Roman government, which was in control of Israel, allowed the Sanhedrin to control Jewish affairs even outside Israel.

1. How are believers described in verse 2?

2. This same designation is used several more times in Acts. (See Acts 19:9, 23; 22:4; 24:14, 22.) To what do you think this designation refers?

3. What did Saul intend to do?

Saul's Conversion (Acts 9:3–9)
Read Acts 9:3–9.
4. Describe what happened to Saul.

5. At what point in this experience do you think Saul was actually converted?

Saul never forgot the amazing, dramatic events that accompanied his conversion. He recounted his experience before a riotous mob in Jerusalem (Acts 22:1–11) and before King Agrippa (Acts 26:1–19). And we may safely assume that he recounted it many more times than the Spirit led Luke to record!

On your Acts Acrostic, add Saul's conversion experience as a Supernatural Event.

Ananias's Concern (Acts 9:10–14, 17–19)
Read Acts 9:10–14.
 6. What kinds of thoughts and feelings do you suppose Saul experienced during the three days he was without sight (v. 9)?

Ananias was a believing Jew. As far as we know, he was not a leader in the church.
 7. What words would you use to describe Ananias?

 8. Name some other Bible characters who were hesitant at first to do what God asked them to do.

The street called Straight in Damascus is thought to be the oldest continually used street in the world. You can still walk down that street today.

Read Acts 9:17–19.
 9. In what ways did Ananias minister to Saul?
   •

   •

   •

   •

10. Notice that Saul was "filled with the Holy Ghost" (v. 17). Review what we learned about the Spirit's ministry (lesson 2). When did Saul receive Spirit baptism and the Spirit's indwelling?

We don't know anything more about Ananias than what we read here in Acts 9. It seems his ministry was limited to one person. You may be discouraged to have only two or three children or teens in your Sunday School class. Perhaps your ladies' Bible study is limited to a very small group. Take heart! Peter preached to thousands in Jerusalem; Philip ministered to a great number of Samaritans; Ananias worked with one man; and Saul . . . You have no idea what God will choose to do with that student or two whom you faithfully teach each week.

Saul's Commission (Acts 9:15, 16)
Read Acts 9:15 and 16.

God encouraged Ananias by letting him know His plans for Saul.

11. What two main things would Saul do?

-

-

Acts 13—28 describe how Saul fulfilled God's commission for him.

Saul's Communication (Acts 9:20–22)
Read Acts 9:20–22.

The converted persecutor wasted no time in starting his ministry.

12. Summarize Saul's message.

13. How did the Jews who heard Saul in the synagogues react?

Saul's Consultation
Read Galatians 1:15–18.

Acts 9:23 says that "after that many days were fulfilled," the Jews sought to kill Saul. "Many days" was a span of about three years. Saul left Damascus and went to the Arabian desert, where he was taught by the Lord Himself (Galatians 1:17). When Saul (Paul) later wrote things like "I have received of the Lord" (1 Corinthians 11:23), he was undoubtedly referring to things he learned from the Lord during those three years of training.

Wilderness experiences are not uncommon for God's servants. Moses spent forty years in Midian before God sent him to Pharaoh. John the Baptist spent time in the wilderness before beginning his public ministry. Even the Lord Jesus Himself had forty days in the wilderness (Matthew 4:1, 2).

14. Read Deuteronomy 8:1–3. Why does God allow a wilderness experience for His people?

The Jews' Conspiracy (Acts 9:23–25)
Read Acts 9:23–25.

15. What happened when Saul returned to Damascus?

16. What did the disciples (believers) in Damascus do?

Barnabas's Commendation (Acts 9:26, 27)
Read Acts 9:26 and 27.

Saul seemed to be readily accepted by the believers in Damascus, but a different situation awaited him when he arrived in Jerusalem some three-plus years after his conversion.

17. How did the believers in Jerusalem react when Saul tried to join them?

We first met Barnabas in Acts 4 (lesson 5). You may recall that his nickname was Son of Consolation or Son of Encouragement.

18. How did Barnabas live up to his nickname in regard to Saul?

Saul's Quiet Years (Acts 9:28–30)
Read Acts 9:28–30.

19. Galatians 1:18 mentions that Saul was in Jerusalem for only fifteen days. According to Acts 9:28 and 29, what did he do during that time?

20. Why and how did Saul leave Jerusalem?

Saul may have stayed in his hometown of Tarsus (Acts 22:3) for eight or nine years. We don't hear of Saul again in Acts until the end of chapter 11.

The Churches' Calm (Acts 9:31)
Read Acts 9:31.

21. Why do you think this was a period of calm for the early believers?

During this time of respite from persecution, the early believers were busy. The text says that the churches were "edified"—that's internal growth. Believers were growing, or maturing, spiritually. The churches also "multiplied"—that's external growth. More churches were started as people continued to come to Christ. What a pattern for churches to emulate today: spiritual maturity on the part of church members and the planting of new churches to aid in the proclamation of the Word. Living day by day in the power of the Spirit produces great results!

Add these Church Facts to your Acts Acrostic: the churches were edified; the churches multiplied.

Apply the Scripture

- Write the details of your conversion experience. If you were saved as a child, you may feel that your experience is rather ho-hum. But it isn't! Thank God that children can understand the gospel message. Thank Him that He preserved you from the sin that might have been part of your life. If you cannot honestly describe a conversion experience, it's not too late to come to Christ. Review the plan of salvation on page 11 and talk to your pastor's wife, Bible study leader, or Christian friend about how you can have this personal relationship with Jesus Christ.

- What are some specific ways you can be an "Ananias" to someone else?

The Gospel for All People

Acts 9:32—10:48

"Then Peter opened his mouth, and said, Of a truth I perceive that God is no respecter of persons" (Acts 10:34).

1. Have you ever been part of a culturally diverse worship service? What was different between that service and the ones you are accustomed to? What could you appreciate about the service?

I've been in African American churches in the U.S., a French-speaking church in France, a Chinese-speaking church in Hong Kong, and an English-speaking church in the Philippines. Each situation had its cultural differences, but each one also enriched my worship in some way.

Someday people of every tribe and nation and language will worship the Lamb on His throne (Revelation 5:9, 10). But the church has not always been one big happy family. As the gospel spread in the years following Jesus' ascension, cultural and racial differences had to be overcome. And that is the focus of this lesson. We return now to the ministry of Peter.

Study the Scripture

Peter Heals Aeneas (Acts 9:32–35)
Read Acts 9:32–35.

Lydda was a large Gentile city about twenty-five miles from Jerusalem. (See the map, resource 2.)

2. What did Peter do in Lydda?

Aeneas was probably an unsaved man, since Luke referred to him as a "certain man" rather than a "certain disciple" (compare verse 33 to verse 36).

Verse 35 does not mean that all people in the area of Lydda and Sharon were converted. Rather, those who heard the testimony of the healed man turned to Christ.

Peter Raises Dorcas (Acts 9:36–43)
Read Acts 9:36–43.

Locate Joppa on the map. It was about ten miles from Lydda. An interesting sidelight: Jonah went to Joppa to escape ministering to Gentiles (Jonah 1:1–3); Peter went to Joppa and began his ministry to the Gentiles.

Dorcas, or Tabitha, was part of the church in Joppa. She was known for her "good works and almsdeeds." We might call this "practical Christianity." Dorcas was a seamstress (v. 39), and she used her skill to care for the needs of others.

3. Compare Mark 5:35–43 to Acts 9:40 and 41. List several similarities between Jesus' raising of Jairus's daughter and Peter's raising of Dorcas.

   •

   •

   •

   •

Verse 43 indicates that Peter stayed in the home of Simon the tanner while he was in Joppa. A tanner had contact with dead bodies. The very fact that Peter would stay with Simon may indicate that Peter was beginning to think outside his Jewish circles.

 Note the healing of Aeneas and the raising of Dorcas as Supernatural Events on your Acts Acrostic.

Peter Takes the Gospel to the Gentiles (Acts 10)

The raising of Dorcas and the events of Acts 10 took place about ten years after Pentecost. Many churches had been established in those ten years, and they were primarily composed of believing Jews. That was about to change.

Read Acts 10:1–8.

Cornelius, a Gentile, was a centurion in the Roman army. A centurion was in charge of one hundred men. He was part of the "Italian band" (v. 1), or "cohort." (Today we might call it a regiment.) A cohort had six hundred men. A Roman "legion" was composed of ten cohorts.

4. What else do we know about Cornelius?

-

-

-

-

Cornelius was probably as close to being a Jewish proselyte as one could be and yet not be one. "He was a model of religious respectability—and yet he was not a saved man."[1]

5. What did an angel of God tell Cornelius to do?

Read Acts 10:9–16.

Meanwhile, in Joppa, Peter was having his own encounter with God as he prayed.

6. Summarize Peter's vision.

God wanted Peter to realize that the Levitical laws concerning clean and unclean animals were no longer valid. God was preparing Peter for the mission he would soon undertake. Indeed, while Peter was on the rooftop, Cornelius's men found the right house in Joppa.

Read Acts 10:17–23.
7. What did the Spirit of God tell Peter to do?

After the men explained their mission, Peter invited them to spend the night. It was too long a journey to return to Caesarea that day. But the next morning, Peter and some men from Joppa (probably Jewish believers; v. 23) left with the men from Caesarea.

Read Acts 10:24–33.
8. (a) How did Cornelius respond when he met Peter?

(b) How did Peter respond?

9. How do you know that after Peter got to Cornelius's home, he understood the meaning of the rooftop vision?

Cornelius then rehearsed for Peter the events on his end that had led to his calling for Peter to come. Cornelius had gathered all his family and his friends (v. 24), and they were ready to hear the message God had given Peter.

Read Acts 10:34–43.
Verses 34 and 35 record some of the most amazing words ever to

come from the mouth of a devout Jew. The Jews were God's Chosen People; He had favored them above all other nations on earth. Now Peter was proclaiming that God was not a respecter of persons: people from any nation could be accepted by Him. This change in Peter's attitude is just another indication of what happens when one is living in the power of the Spirit.

10. Read John 10:16. How did Peter's encounter with Cornelius fulfill the words of Christ?

Verse 35 has sometimes been taken to mean that salvation is by works. But "accepted with him" is the not the same as "saved." Cornelius needed to be saved, according to Acts 11:14. The idea is that God's favor is available to both Jews and Gentiles.

11. Peter's sermon highlighted the life of Christ. What events or themes are included in these verses?

Verse 37

Verse 38

Verse 39

Verse 40

Verses 41, 42

Read Acts 10:44–48.

12. What happened when Peter completed his message?

Verse 44

Verse 46

Verses 47, 48

13. How did the Jews who accompanied Peter respond?

Peter and the Keys to the Kingdom
Read Matthew 16:13–19.

This passage does not establish Peter as the founder of the church or the first pope. The "rock" Jesus mentioned (v. 18) was undoubtedly Peter's great confession concerning Christ (v. 16). The proper recognition of Who Jesus is became the foundation of the church. However, Peter was given "keys" to the kingdom. Many Bible scholars see the fulfillment of this gift in the book of Acts.

14. In each of the following passages, note the group to whom the gospel was given.

    Key No. 1
    Acts 2:14–40

    Peter preached the gospel to the _____.

    Key No. 2
    Acts 8:14–17

    Peter confirmed that the gospel had been preached to the

    _____ .

    Key No. 3
    Acts 10

    Peter took the gospel to the _____.

In all three of these instances, the coming of the Holy Spirit is mentioned as a specific event. With the Jews and the Gentiles, the coming of the Spirit was accompanied by speaking in other languages (Acts 2:4; 10:46). That may have happened in Samaria as well, but Scripture does not record it.

Peter's use of the keys authenticated the inclusion of each group in the church, the Body of Christ. The door was now open to all people!

Peter stayed with Cornelius and the other new believers for a few days—perhaps so he could fulfill the "teaching" part of the Great Commission (Matthew 28:20).

 *If you have not already done so, note these items on your Acts Acrostic: The Holy Spirit given to the Gentiles (**A**ctions of the Holy Spirit); Gentiles added to the church; new believers baptized (**C**hurch Facts); new believers spoke in other languages (**T**ransitional Details); Cornelius's and Peter's visions (**S**upernatural Events).*

Apply the Scripture

- Dorcas used her ability as a seamstress to display "practical Christianity." What kinds of things would you consider "practical Christianity" today? More specifically, how do you live out your Christianity in a practical way?
- Read Galatians 3:26–29 and Ephesians 2:11–20. Because we are two millennia removed from the events of Acts 10 and because we are most likely Gentiles, it is hard to realize what a momentous event Acts 10 presents. Thank God that you did not need to become a Jewish proselyte to become a Christian. Thank Him that He is no respecter of people. Thank Him that the gospel is available to all and for all!
- Because we have the complete revelation of God, our Bible, God does not make His will known to us in visions (though sometimes we wish He did!). But the Holy Spirit does prompt us to do certain things. He may prompt you to speak a word of witness to someone, to give out a tract, to assure someone of your prayers, to exercise your practical Christianity. Do not ignore these divine promptings. Be as ready to obey God as both Peter and Cornelius were.

Note

1. Wiersbe, 126.

LESSON 12

Called "Christians"

Acts 11

"When they heard these things, they held their peace, and glorified God, saying, Then hath God also to the Gentiles granted repentance unto life" (Acts 11:18).

Have you ever had someone "rain on your parade"? You know what that is: you are all excited about something you've heard or done or experienced, and the person with whom you share your excitement quickly dampens your enthusiasm with negative comments or observations. Acts 11 records some Jews in Jerusalem giving Peter the rain-on-your-parade treatment.

Study the Scripture

Peter Goes to Jerusalem (Acts 11:1–18)
Read Acts 11:1–4.

Eventually the report of the conversion of the Gentile Cornelius and his household in Caesarea reached Jerusalem. Peter was called to give an explanation.

"They that were of the circumcision" (v. 2) were Jews. The term may refer to a group known as the "circumcision party," a legalistic group of Jewish converts. They were followers of Christ, but they continued to think some aspects of Judaism should be retained.

1. What word is used to describe the Jews' reaction to Peter?

2. These Jews were really upset with Peter. What did they say he had done?

3. What does eating with someone signify or symbolize?

4. Read Mark 2:16 and Luke 15:2. Who else had been rebuked for eating with sinners?

Acts 11 provides another glimpse of church life in the church's infancy. The believers in Jerusalem were quite willing to confront Peter. Peter, however, did not "pull rank" in answering them. The people functioned in a way consistent with congregational government.

Read Acts 11:5–15.
  5. What event is recounted in these verses?

Note the phrase "all thy house," or household, in verse 14. This term in Acts always means people in the home who were old enough to believe. The household could include the immediate family, relatives, and even household slaves.

"At the beginning" in verse 15 refers to the beginning of this new work God was doing; that is, Pentecost. The Holy Spirit came on the Gentile believers in Cornelius's home just as He had come on the Jews at Pentecost (Acts 2).

Read Acts 11:16–18.
Peter finalized his argument by saying that since God had given the Holy Spirit to the Jews, how could he stand in the way of God's giving the Holy Spirit to the Gentiles (v. 17)?

Read verse 18 again; it is the key verse for this lesson. John MacArthur calls this "one of the most shocking admissions in Jewish history":[1] God has granted repentance to the Gentiles!
  6. Look at verses 2 and 18 again. What progression of emotions/actions is recorded on the part of the Jews?

Sometimes we forget that reconciliation is one of the components of the gospel. A person who believes is reconciled to God (Romans 5:10;

2 Corinthians 5:18–20)—the vertical dimension of reconciliation. Often, however, salvation also provides horizontal reconciliation—person to person. We see that happening here in Acts 11. Jews and Gentiles, living in the power of the Spirit, learned to get along as members of the Body of Christ.

 *Record the Holy Spirit's coming on the Gentiles as an Act of the Holy Spirit on your Acts Acrostic. The Jews' acceptance of the Gentiles could be recorded as a **Church Fact**.*

Barnabas and Saul Go to Antioch (11:19–26)
Read Acts 11:19–21.

Verses 19–21 describe what was happening in the north at the same time as the ministries in Samaria and Caesarea.

The persecution that led to Stephen's death (Acts 7) also resulted in believers leaving Jerusalem (Acts 8:4).

7. To what places did these scattered believers go (Acts 11:19)? Locate these areas on the map (resource 2).

At first only Jews were being evangelized (v. 19); the news of what happened in Caesarea had not yet reached Antioch. But then converts from places like Cyprus and Cyrene started to preach to the Hellenist Jews (or "Grecians"), who probably lived more like Greeks than like Jews.

8. What was the result of this evangelistic effort?

Antioch was the third largest city in the Roman Empire at that time. (Only Rome and Alexandria were larger.) Half a million people lived in Antioch. The city was situated on a river, giving it an outlet to the Mediterranean Sea just sixteen miles away at Seleucia. Antioch was three hundred miles north of Jerusalem with a large Jewish population and many Jewish proselytes. (Nicolas, one of the Seven in Acts 6, was a Jewish proselyte from Antioch.)

Antioch was a wealthy city. The main street was four miles long and paved with marble. Marble colonnades lined the street, which was lit at night. But the city was also grossly immoral. The temple of Daphne, where ritual prostitution was practiced, was only five miles away.

We note here an important missions principle from the book of Acts: the evangelization of the city. The great cities of the day were evangelized by the early church. After a strong church was established in a large city, it was easier to reach out to the surrounding areas. In our day, large cities have been mostly abandoned by Bible-believing, Bible-preaching churches. What, do you suppose, could be the correlation between the decay of urban areas and the absence of the true church?

Read Acts 11:22–26.

9. What happened when the church in Jerusalem heard about the work God was doing in Antioch?

10. Barnabas was from the island of Cyprus, about one hundred miles off the coast of Antioch. What do you remember about Barnabas from earlier studies in Acts?

    •

    •

    •

11. What else do we learn about Barnabas in verses 23 and 24?

    •

    •

    •

Barnabas must have recognized that the work in Antioch was

greater than one man could handle. Whether or not Barnabas had kept in touch with Saul during the seven to ten years Saul was in Tarsus, we do not know. But Barnabas recognized Saul's abilities, so Barnabas went to Tarsus to get Saul.

12. When the men got back to Antioch, what did they do?

13. What interesting fact do we learn in verse 26?

The name "Christian" was a term of derision. It meant "belonging to the party of Christ." The title was probably given by non-Jews to believers since Jews would have hesitated to use the name of Messiah in this way. The word is used only two other times in the New Testament: Acts 26:28 and 1 Peter 4:16.

Barnabas and Saul Go to Jerusalem (Acts 11:27–30)
Read Acts 11:27–30.

14. What news did the prophet Agabus bring to the church at Antioch?

15. What is the difference between the way this need was met and the way needs recorded in Acts 4:34–37 were met?

After the offering was collected, Barnabas and Saul took it to the church in Jerusalem so the church leaders could deliver help to those who needed it. Living by the power of the Spirit, believers in the early church were eager to help others.

*Note these truths under **Church Facts** on your Acts Acrostic: disciples first called Christians; one church sent relief to another church. A **Transitional Detail** is the New Testament gift of prophecy.*

Apply the Scripture

- Review the way Peter answered the Jews in Jerusalem. What can you learn from him about ways to work with people who may see an issue differently than you do?

- Think about the current use of the word "Christian." How does its current use differ from the original use? If you identify yourself to someone as a Christian, do you think that person realizes what you mean? What might be a better way to identify yourself?

- What kinds of situations might necessitate one church sending an offering to another church? What safeguards should be in place before such an offering is given to another church?

Note

   1.   MacArthur, 60.

Persistent Prayer

Acts 12

"Peter therefore was kept in prison: but prayer was made without ceasing of the church unto God for him" (Acts 12:5).

1. What kinds of things are on your prayer list? Recall a recent answer to prayer. Was the answer what you expected? How persistently did you pray for this request?

2. Now think of times your church gathers for prayer. What answers has your church experienced?

Alfred, Lord Tennyson wrote, "More things are wrought by prayer than this world dreams of." Yet the church—who should know more about prayer than anyone else—often fails to use this potent resource. But not the early church; prayer was their only recourse, and they used it mightily.

Study the Scripture

Herod's Rage (Acts 12:1–4)
Read Acts 12:1–4.

The Herodian family is prominent in Acts, so it helps to understand which Herod was which. If you look at resource 7, you will have a better idea of the relationship between the Herods.

Herod the Great ruled in Israel from 37 to 4 BC. He was from the area known as Idumea. (Idumea was the Greek/Roman name for the despised country of Edom.) He was appointed king of the Jews by the Roman government. He was the Herod when Jesus was born (Matthew 2:1). He was a ruthless ruler, killing his own wife, several sons and other relatives, and, of course, the baby boys in a wide area after Jesus' birth. He also restored the temple and built many buildings in Jerusalem. He built the city and harbor of Caesarea. He was ravaged by disease and died at his palace in Jericho in 4 BC.

Herod Antipas, a son of Herod the Great, was the ruler who imprisoned and beheaded John the Baptist (Matthew 14:1–10). He was married to Herodias, his half brother's wife.

Herod Agrippa I is the Herod of Acts 12. He was a grandson of Herod the Great. He ruled in Israel from AD 37 to 44. He was part Jewish, and he did all he could to curry the favor of the Jews. Some additional members of the Herodian family are mentioned later in Acts.

3. What did Herod Agrippa I do?

4. What James is this? Read Matthew 4:21.

James was the first of the Twelve to suffer a martyr's death, and his is the only death of an apostle recorded in the New Testament.

The Feast of Unleavened Bread was celebrated for seven days after Passover (Leviticus 23:5, 6). When Acts 12:4 refers to bringing Peter to trial "after Easter" (that is, Passover), Luke was referring to the entire eight-day celebration.

A "quaternion" is a squad of four soldiers. One squad was assigned to Peter for each of the four watches of the night. Two soldiers in each squad were chained to Peter; two stood guard.

The Church's Recourse (Acts 12:5, 12)
Read Acts 12:5 and 12.

5. What do you think the church prayed for?

6. Where was this prayer meeting held?

Church tradition says this was the home where Jesus celebrated the Last Supper with His disciples and where the disciples met between the Ascension and Pentecost (Acts 1:12, 13).

The prayer meeting in Mary's home may have been going on for as long as a week, considering that the Feast of Unleavened Bread lasted an entire week.

Peter's Release (Acts 12:6–19)
Read Acts 12:6–10.

7. The release happened the night before Herod was planning to take Peter from prison and probably to kill him. What was Peter doing?

Doctor Luke, the writer of Acts, gave interesting insights into what people did in prison. Peter slept. Paul and Silas sang (Acts 16).

8. What happened while Peter was sleeping?

An old Puritan preacher, Thomas Watson, said, "The angel fetched Peter out of prison, but it was prayer that fetched the angel!"

This account is a good example of the divine-human cooperative. God does the extraordinary, the supernatural; people do the ordinary.

9. What did God do that Peter could not do?

•

•

•

10. What could Peter do for himself that God did not do?

•

•

•

Read Acts 12:11–17.

11. What happened when Peter got to the house where he evidently knew the church would be gathered?

The James in verse 17 is the half-brother of Jesus. It seems that he had become the leader of the church in Jerusalem. Peter wanted to make sure James knew about his release. (The fact that James was not with the group at Mary's house is evidence that the church in Jerusalem met together in many different locations due to the size of the church.)

After this brief meeting with the believers in Mary's house, Peter departed. Luke did not record where he went. However, Acts 15 records an important meeting in Jerusalem, and Peter was there. But other than that occasion, Peter is no longer a prominent figure in Acts. He may have had an itinerant ministry with his wife. ("Cephas" in 1 Corinthians 9:5 is Peter.) It is possible that Peter *never* went to Rome, since Paul did not mention him in Romans. Peter wrote two letters to persecuted, scattered believers during the persecution under Nero around AD 64. He died as a martyr about AD 67; tradition says he was crucified upside down.

Living in the power of the Spirit changed Peter from a cowardly disciple at the time of the Crucifixion to the major leader in the church in Jerusalem during the first decades of its existence.

 Record Peter's miraculous release from prison as a Supernatural Event on your Acts Acrostic.

Read Acts 12:18 and 19.

12. What happened when Herod could not find Peter the next day?

13. Where did Herod go?

Herod's Reckoning (Acts 12:20–24)
Read Acts 12:20–24.

There had been a dispute between Herod and the cities of Tyre and Sidon. Evidently the dispute was settled, so Herod decided to mark the occasion with a grand speech.

14. How did the people respond to Herod's speech?

Josephus, the first-century Jewish historian, said Herod's royal robes were made of silver so they sparkled in the sun. Undoubtedly this glistening sight only further ignited the crowd.

15. What happened to Herod?

16. Read 1 Peter 3:12, words of Old Testament Scripture that Peter wrote to persecuted believers. What might Peter have had in mind?

No power can triumph over the Word of God. Those who attempt to harm God's people will, in the end, face judgment themselves. Acts 12 begins with a persecuted church and a strong Herod; it ends with a strong church and a dead Herod!

 *Record another **Supernatural Event:** the death of Herod.*

Verse 24 is a summary verse, and then verse 25 introduces the rest of the book of Acts. Barnabas and Sau' went back to Antioch, and John Mark went with them. The study of Acts 13—20 is the subject of the study guide *Serving in the Power of the Spirit.*

Apply the Scripture

- This chapter is a reminder of how far we have come from the model of the early church when it comes to prayer. What would happen if we met to pray—and only pray—well into the night for the concerns of our church? What if we met to pray for even one solid hour? Do we shortchange what God does in our midst because we pray so little?

- As we have mentioned in previous lessons, the number of persecuted believers today is great. Read Hebrews 13:3 and consider how that verse relates to prayer for the persecuted church. List some specific requests you can bring before the Lord for persecuted believers. (Compare your list to the suggestions in the answers section of this book.)
- We learn something about God's sovereign choices in Acts 12. His ways are higher than our ways (Isaiah 55:8, 9), and His ways are often beyond our understanding (Romans 11:33). James was killed, but Peter was released. This was God's sovereign choice. It is not a statement about the men's spirituality, usefulness to the church, or anything else. We must not compare God's dealings with one person with His dealings with another person. He is God. We must trust His ways.

Leader's Guide

Suggestions for Leaders

Studying the Bible is one of our greatest joys as believers. With Jeremiah the prophet we can say, "Thy words were found, and I did eat them; and thy word was unto me the joy and rejoicing of mine heart" (Jeremiah 15:16). The psalmist said, "I will delight myself in thy statutes: I will not forget thy word" (Psalm 119:16), and, "The statutes of the LORD are right, rejoicing the heart: the commandment of the LORD is pure, enlightening the eyes" (Psalm 19:8). As a Bible study leader, you have the opportunity to lead women in discovering the joy of studying and applying God's Word.

The effectiveness of a group Bible study usually depends on two things: (1) the leader herself, and (2) the ladies' commitment to prepare beforehand and interact during the study. You cannot totally control the second factor, but you have total control over the first one. These brief suggestions will help you be an effective Bible study leader.

You will want to prepare each lesson a week in advance. During the week, read supplemental material and look for illustrations in the everyday events of your life as well as in the lives of others.

This particular study has additional resources that are available online. Read pages 9 and 10. You may choose to copy the resources and distribute them to all the ladies in the group. Note that each lady will need thirteen copies of resource 1.

Resource 1 is an aid to Bible study. It gives you and your group members specific things to look for as you study each lesson's Scripture passage. The entries each week will vary somewhat from member to member. But certain things should be recorded by all the members. These items are noted with the designation in the lesson itself.

Encourage the ladies in the Bible study to complete each lesson before the meeting. This preparation will make the discussion more interesting. You can suggest that ladies answer two or three questions a day as part of their daily Bible reading rather than trying to do the entire lesson at one sitting.

You may also want to encourage the ladies to memorize the key verse for each lesson. (This is the verse that is printed in italics at the start of each lesson.) If possible, print the verses on 3" x 5" cards to distribute each week. If you cannot do this, suggest that the ladies make their own cards and keep them in a prominent place throughout the week.

The physical setting in which you meet will have some bearing on the study itself. An informal circle of chairs, chairs around a table, someone's living room or family room—these types of settings encourage people to relax and participate. In addition to an informal setting, create an atmosphere in which ladies feel free to participate and be themselves.

Observe these basic guidelines during times of discussion:

- Don't do all the talking yourself. This study is not designed to be a lecture.
- Encourage discussion by giving ladies time to think and formulate answers.
- Don't discuss controversial issues that will divide the group. (Differences of opinion are healthy; divisions are not.)
- Don't let one lady dominate the discussion. Use statements such as these to draw others into the study: "Let's hear from someone on this side of the room" (the side opposite the dominant talker); "Let's hear from someone who has not shared yet today."
- Stay on the subject. The tendency toward tangents is always possible in a discussion. One of your responsibilities as the leader is to keep the group on track.
- Don't get bogged down on a question that interests only one person.

Knowing what the Scripture teaches is never an end in itself, or else we are in danger of being hearers only and not doers of the Word (James 1:22). Take time each week to consider the "Apply the Scripture" suggestions. Adapt the printed suggestions or add to them to make them applicable to your group members.

God bless you as you lead this study!

Answers for Leader's Use

Information inside parentheses ( ) is additional instruction for the group leader.

Lesson 1

1. Personal answers.

2. Possible questions include, How did the church start? How did the Holy Spirit come? What happened to Peter and the other apostles? Who is Paul? What was the first church like? How did the gospel get all the way to Rome?

3. Luke was the writer; he also wrote the Gospel of Luke.

4. The pronouns are plural.

5. Luke was a physician.

6. Restore the kingdom to Israel.

7. The Holy Spirit would come.

8. A witness tells what she knows or has experienced.

9. Personal answers. (Lead the ladies to see that even casual comments such as, "I'm having a terrible day" can open the door for a response such as, "I know what you mean. I don't know what I would do if I didn't have the Lord to help me.")

10. Jesus had to leave so the Holy Spirit could come.

11. Jesus lifted off the earth until He was covered with a cloud and the disciples could no longer see Him. Two men—probably angels—appeared to the disciples and explained that Jesus had gone back to Heaven and that He would one day return in the same way they had seen Him go.

12. They went to an upper room—perhaps the same one in which they had hid after the Resurrection (John 20:19). Included in the group were a number of women, one of whom was Jesus' mother, Mary. His "brethren" were also present. This is a reference to Jesus' half-brothers who had come to believe that He is Who He had said He is.

13. The man needed to know of the Lord's ministry from the beginning, and he needed to have seen the resurrected Christ.

14. They prayed and then cast lots.

Lesson 2

1. (a) Feast of Passover. (b) Feast of Unleavened Bread. (c) Another feast, known as the Feast of Weeks (because it lasted seven full weeks, or fifty days), or the Feast of Firstfruits, because the new grain was offered to the Lord.

2. The sound of a mighty wind; tongues as of fire; speaking in known languages.

3. Three possible themes are (1) Jesus is the promised Messiah; (2) Jesus died and rose again; (3) you are guilty and need to repent and be saved.

4. "His body," that is, the Body of Christ.

5. The church is not a building (even though we commonly use that word for the building). The church is people. (The Greek word *ekklesia* means "called-out assembly.")

6. "They continued stedfastly in the apostles' doctrine."

7. Personal answers.

8. Fellowship. ("Fellowship"; "breaking of bread"; "had all things common.")

9. Personal answers.

10. Personal answers.

11. People are united; they are happy together; people are saved.

Lesson 3

1. Peter and John were going to the temple at the ninth hour, which would be 3 p.m. (The first hour was 6 a.m.)

2. Over 40 years old.

3. The man asked for alms. Peter said he didn't have any money, but he had something else. He commanded the man to walk in the name of Jesus of Nazareth.

4. We avoid eye contact.

5. (a) Saved; (b) life; (c) baptized; (d) pray; (e) give thanks; (f) help (hope); (g) help others; (h) little children.

6. "Feet and ankle bones received strength"; "leaping up"; "stood, and walked"; "walking, and leaping."

7. The crowd thought the apostles were drunk.

8. The apostles had done the miracle in their own power.

9. Isaiah.

10. Deuteronomy 18:18–20.

11. Samuel—and all the prophets after him.

12. His Son Jesus (v. 13); the Holy One (v. 14); the Just (v. 14); the Prince of life (v. 15); the Christ (v. 18); Jesus Christ (v. 20); Prophet (vv. 22, 23); His Son Jesus (v. 26).

Lesson 4

1. They seized the apostles (Peter and John, continuing from chapter 3). They did it in the evening.

2. Five thousand.

3. It is an exclusive verse. There is NO OTHER WAY to Heaven except through Jesus Christ. Today people want to believe that many roads lead to Heaven.

4. As unlearned and ignorant.

5. The Sanhedrin couldn't deny the miracle, but they feared a riot if they punished the apostles.

6. They were commanded to not speak or teach in the name of Jesus.

7. The apostles had to obey God and continue to tell what they had seen and heard.

8. When the decree contradicts God's law.

9. Some examples are the Hebrew midwives (Exodus 1:15–21); the three Hebrew young men (Daniel 3); Daniel (Daniel 6).

10. Psalm 2.

11. Personal answers.

12. "Do whatsoever thy hand and thy counsel determined before to be done."

13. Boldness.

Lesson 5

1. The believers sold their possessions and shared with other believers.

2. The Jews were to leave some of their harvest for the poor and the stranger in their midst. They were to "open thine hand wide" to the poor among them.

3. The needy.

4. His given name was Joses (Joseph); his nickname was Barnabas; "Barnabas" means "son of consolation" or encouragement; he was a Levite; his home was on the island of Cyprus; he owned land; he sold land; he gave the proceeds to the apostles.

5. The couple sold some land. They kept some of the money for themselves, but when they took the rest to the apostles, they represented the amount as being the total sale.

6. Lying to the Holy Spirit.

7. Tempting or testing the Holy Spirit.

8. (a) Pride. (b) How generous they were.

9. Romans 12:3—Don't think more highly of yourself than you should. Proverbs 11:2—Pride brings shame. Proverbs 16:18—Pride brings destruction. Proverbs 6:16, 17—Pride is one of the seven things named as being an abomination to the Lord. 1 Peter 5:5—God resists the proud.

10. Ananias died immediately. Sapphira went to Peter about three hours later. She confirmed that the price was correct, and she died.

11. (Ask two or three ladies to share their ideas.)

12. They were devoured by fire from the Lord and died.

13. Achan took some of the forbidden plunder from Jericho; he and his family were stoned and burned to death.

14. Great fear came upon the church.

Apply: Suggestions could include special gifts from individuals; special gifts from the church; help from the church's benevolent fund; donating time and talents to help.

Lesson 6

1. (Ask two or three ladies to share their experiences.)

2. The death of Ananias and Sapphira for lying to the Holy Spirit.

3. Answers should include signs and wonders done by the church; multitudes of new believers; healing of sick and demon-possessed people.

4. Acts 5:12 is the answer to the prayer of Acts 4:30.

5. People were healed by simply having Peter's shadow pass over them.

6. The indwelling Holy Spirit helps us understand God's Word.

7. A primary reason is that Peter and John had disobeyed the order previously

given to them (Acts 4:17). Other possible reasons include jealousy or envy on the part of the religious leaders and the fact that the religious leaders were losing their power over the people.

8. An angel opened the prison doors and led the apostles out.

9. They went to the temple early in the morning and taught the people.

10. "We found a well-guarded cell, but the prisoners were not in the cell."

11. "The men you put in prison are teaching in the temple."

12. Filled Jerusalem with their doctrine, or teaching.

13. (a) "His blood be on us, and on our children." (b) The crowd was testifying to the death of an innocent Man.

14. The men wanted to kill the apostles.

15. He gave two examples of men who had caused uprisings. Then he advised the council to leave the men alone. If their activity was just from man, it wouldn't last; if it was from God, they couldn't stop it anyway.

16. Beat the apostles and commanded them to stop speaking in Jesus' name.

17. They rejoiced that they were considered worthy of persecution, and they continued preaching daily.

Lesson 7

1. Grecians and Hebrews.

2. The Hebrews may have thought they were better Jews than the Grecians; the Grecians may have considered themselves more enlightened.

3. The Grecians said the Hebrews were neglecting Grecian widows in the daily "ministration."

4. The distribution of money or goods to those who had need.

5. The apostles ("the twelve") called the meeting. They didn't want to shortchange their ministry in teaching God's Word to care for these other needs.

6. We are to honor widows. Caring for widows is an indication of pure, or undefiled, religion.

7. A good reputation; filling (control) of the Holy Spirit; wisdom.

8. A good reputation would indicate that the men were not partial to one side or the other. Being filled with the Spirit was an evidence of their spirituality. Handling the situation correctly called for wisdom.

9. Prayed and laid hands on them.

10. Only two: Stephen and Philip.

11. The Word of God spread; the number of believers multiplied greatly; many priests believed.

12. Full of faith; full of power; did great wonders and miracles.

13. Blasphemy against Moses, against God, and against the temple.

14. His face looked like the face of an angel.

Lesson 8

1. The numbers should be in this order: 12, 5, 10, 14, 1, 9, 2, 11, 3, 8, 13, 7, 4, 15, 6.

2. Stephen had gone to the synagogue of the freedmen to present the gospel. This

upset the Jews, who had him taken to the Sanhedrin, or council. The high priest asked Stephen if the blasphemy charges against him were true.

3. The God of glory.

4. The glory of God.

5. (1) God appeared to Abraham in Mesopotamia before he went to Haran; (2) God told Abraham to leave his country; (3) Abraham went to Haran; when his father died, he moved on to Canaan; (4) God promised to give the land to Abraham's seed even though he had no child at the time; (5) Abraham's seed would be in bondage in a different country for four hundred years; (6) God gave Abraham the covenant of circumcision.

6. (1) Joseph's envious brothers sold Joseph into Egypt; (2) God was with Joseph; (3) God gave Joseph favor in Pharaoh's sight; (4) Pharaoh made Joseph governor over Egypt; (5) famine came to the lands of Canaan and Egypt; (6) Jacob sent his sons to Egypt; (7) on the second visit, Joseph revealed his identity; (8) Joseph brought his father and all the household to Egypt, where Jacob died.

7. The Hebrews multiplied greatly. They were treated with great cruelty, even to the point of losing their children.

8. (1) Moses spent three months in his own home; (2) he was then raised as the son of Pharaoh's daughter; (3) he was a well-educated Egyptian; (4) he went to check on his Hebrew kinsmen when he was forty years old; (5) his killing of an Egyptian who was oppressing a Hebrew was misunderstood by his people; (6) Moses fled to Midian, where he married a wife and had two sons.

9. (1) He experienced the burning bush; (2) God sent Moses to Egypt to deliver the people.

10. (1) God delivered the people from Egypt, across the Red Sea, and through forty years in the wilderness; (2) God gave the law to Moses on Mount Sinai; (3) the people rejected God and made a golden calf; (4) the Israelites had the tabernacle in the wilderness, as God had commanded Moses.

11. Joshua ("Jesus"), David, Solomon.

12. (1) You have resisted the Holy Spirit (v. 51); (2) your ancestors killed God's prophets (v. 52); (3) you betrayed and murdered the Just One (v. 52); (4) you have not obeyed the law (v. 53).

13. The "trials" of the two men were not held according to Jewish law; both were accused of blasphemy (Matthew 26:65); a riotous mob was involved in both situations; false witnesses were used in both cases (Matthew 26:60).

14. His name means "crown"; as a martyr, he received the crown of life.

15. The writer of Hebrews said Jesus is seated in Heaven; Stephen saw Jesus standing.

16. Perhaps Jesus stands to welcome His children Home to Heaven.

17. His death energized the early church; it continued to grow, not shrink. So the enemies of the church were all the more incensed.

18. The believers scattered from Jerusalem, and they took the gospel message wherever they went.

Lesson 9

1. Philip the evangelist.

2. Jews had no dealings with Samaritans.

3. Jesus said His followers should be His witnesses in Samaria.

4. People were saved; people were healed; the city was filled with joy.

5. He was a sorcerer.

6. Simon believed, was baptized, and became enamored with the miracles Philip was able to perform.

7. The church in Jerusalem heard about the many conversions in Samaria.

8. They prayed that the Samaritan believers would receive the Holy Spirit.

9. Simon wanted to pay Peter to give him the Holy Spirit. Peter rebuked Simon for thinking the gift of God could be purchased with money.

10. Personal answers. (It appears that Simon's confession [v. 13] was not genuine. He seemed to be drawn to the ability to do miracles and the supernatural aspect of the apostles' ministry.)

11. God sent Philip to a deserted area, a road from Jerusalem to Gaza through barren conditions.

12. An Ethiopian eunuch who was the treasurer for Candace, queen of Ethiopia. He had gone to Jerusalem to worship and was returning home. He was reading the scroll of Isaiah.

13. Philip asked him a question. (A helpful book on the use of questions in helping people come to Christ is *Ask Them Why* by Jay Lucas, published by Regular Baptist Press.)

14. Isaiah 53.

15. Be baptized.

16. If the man truly believed that Jesus is the Son of God.

17. The Ethiopian went on his way rejoicing; the Spirit caught Philip away and took him to a new ministry.

Lesson 10

1. People of "this way."

2. John 14:6 refers to Jesus as "the way." Undoubtedly the early Christians emphasized that Jesus is the only way to God and Heaven.

3. Round up believers in Damascus, bind them, and bring them back to Jerusalem, where they would endure further persecution.

4. As Saul was traveling with his companions, he saw a light that was bright enough to knock him to the ground. He heard the Lord speak to him. He acknowledged that the voice was that of the Lord, and he responded by asking the Lord what He wanted Saul to do. When Saul arose from the earth, he was blind.

5. Probably at the time he acknowledged, "Who art thou, Lord?" and "Lord, what wilt thou have me to do?"

6. Maybe he thought of the people he had persecuted and even killed. Maybe he thought of Old Testament Scriptures concerning the Messiah, Whom He had now met.

7. Possible answers are humble, layperson, submissive.

8. Moses (Exodus 3; 4); Gideon (Judges 6); Jeremiah (Jeremiah 1); even Jonah (Jonah 1).

9. (1) Ananias laid his hands on Saul, and Saul received his sight; (2) he made sure Saul had food; (3) he either baptized Saul himself or took Saul to someone who baptized him; (4) he introduced Saul to the disciples (believers) in Damascus.

10. When he was converted.

11. Bear God's name before Gentiles, kings, and Jews; suffer for His name's sake.

12. Jesus is the Messiah, the Son of God.

13. They were amazed. They recognized Saul as the former persecutor.

14. To humble us and test us; to know if we are truly going to obey and follow Him; to teach us to depend on Him.

15. The Jews conspired to kill Saul.

16. They put Saul in a basket and let him down over the city wall at night.

17. They were afraid of him and did not believe he was a genuine believer.

18. Barnabas went with Saul to a gathering of the Jerusalem believers and recounted Saul's conversion experience for them.

19. He was preaching boldly, and he was discussing, or disputing, with the Grecian Jews (undoubtedly about the gospel).

20. The Jews wanted to kill Saul, so the believers took him to the coastal city of Caesarea. From there Saul went to Tarsus.

21. Probably because the chief persecutor had been converted!

Lesson 11

1. (Ask several ladies to share their experiences.)

2. He healed Aeneas, a man who had been bedridden with palsy for eight years.

3. (1) Both were women; (2) the rooms where the bodies lay were filled with mourners; (3) similar words were used ("Talitha, arise" and "Tabitha, arise"); (4) both Jesus and Peter held the hand of the woman: Jesus before the miracle of resurrection and Peter just after it.

4. (1) He was devout, or religious; (2) he and his household feared God; (3) he gave to the poor; (4) he was a man of prayer.

5. Send men to Joppa to find Peter.

6. Peter saw a variety of animals and birds; he heard a voice telling him to kill and eat. Peter refused because the animals and birds were "unclean" for a Jew. (See the commands in Leviticus 11.) Three times Peter heard the same command.

7. Go down to the door and meet the men.

8. (a) Cornelius fell at Peter's feet and worshiped him. (b) Peter told Cornelius to stand up; Peter was a man like Cornelius.

9. Peter said the vision helped him understand that he should not call any man common or unclean (v. 28).

10. Jesus told the disciples that He had to bring "other sheep" into His fold; that is, others who were not Jews. Peter was taking the gospel to those "other sheep."

11. Verse 37—Jesus' baptism; verse 38—Jesus' ministry; verse 39—Jesus' death; verse 40—Jesus' resurrection; verses 41, 42—Jesus' post-resurrection ministry.

12. Verse 44—The Holy Spirit came upon the listeners; verse 46—they spoke in other languages; verses 47, 48—they were baptized.

13. They were astonished.

14. Jews; Samaritans; Gentiles.

Lesson 12

1. "Contended."

2. The Jews said Peter had eaten with Gentiles.

3. Acceptance; fellowship.

4. Jesus.

5. Peter's rooftop vision, his visit to Cornelius, and Cornelius's response.

6. First they were contentious; then they were silent ("held their peace"); finally, they glorified God.

7. Phenice, Cyprus, Antioch (of Pisidia).

8. A great number of people believed and turned to the Lord.

9. The Jerusalem church sent Barnabas to the Antioch church.

10. Barnabas's nickname was "son of consolation" ("encourager"); he sold his land and gave the proceeds to the apostles; he introduced Saul to the believers in Jerusalem.

11. (1) Barnabas was glad for all that God had done; (2) he encouraged the believers to "cleave" to the Lord; (3) he was a good man; (4) he was full of the Holy Spirit and faith.

12. For an entire year Barnabas and Saul met with the church as "teachers in residence."

13. The disciples—followers of Christ—were first called "Christians" in Antioch.

14. A famine would occur and cover a large area.

15. The disciples in Antioch (Acts 11) gave an offering according to their ability; the disciples in Jerusalem (Acts 4) sold their land and gave the proceeds to the apostles; the apostles distributed to the people with need.

Lesson 13

1. (Ask two or three ladies to share a recent answer to prayer.)

2. (Talk together about answers to prayer your church has experienced.)

3. Herod killed James.

4. The brother of John; the son of Zebedee. James and John were fishermen, and they were the first two disciples Jesus called.

5. We usually assume the church prayed for Peter's release. But because of the great surprise on the part of the people when he was released, it seems probable this was *not* the primary request. They may have prayed that Peter would face suffering and death like Stephen did. They may have prayed that he would be a bold witness. They may have prayed that he would not deny the Lord as he had done at Jesus' crucifixion (Matthew 26:69–75).

6. In the home of Mary, the mother of John Mark.

7. Sleeping.

8. The angel came to him, and a light shone around him. The angel touched Peter's side and told him to get up and get dressed and then follow him out of the prison.

9. (1) Loosened the chains; (2) immobilized the guards; (3) opened the iron gate.

10. (1) Put on his shoes; (2) put on his clothes; (3) walked out the door.

11. Rhoda, the servant girl, recognized Peter by his voice, but in her excitement and haste, she failed to open the gate. When she ran to tell the people that Peter had been released, they did not believe her. Peter kept knocking until at last someone let him in.

12. The guards were killed, which was a typical Roman practice when condemned prisoners escaped.

13. To Caesarea, the city built by his grandfather.

14. They cried out, "It is the voice of a god, and not of a man."

15. God smote him with a severe intestinal disease, and he died.

16. The prayer that was offered to God on his behalf and then the death of Herod.

Apply: That they will have grace to endure persecution; that they will have opportunities to witness to guards and fellow prisoners; that they will be encouraged by meditating on the Word of God; that they will have wisdom in dealing with their captives; that their families will be strengthened and comforted; that God will grant deliverance, if that is His will.

Resource 3

1. Gideon; Samson; Saul; David; Azariah; Zechariah; Ezekiel.
2. Saul; Samson.
3. Not depart.
4. Indwells.
5. Sealed.
6. Baptized.
7. Gifts; fills.
8. Quench; grieve.

Resource 5

Part A

1. He pronounced repeated woes on the Pharisees.
2. Whitewashed graves.
3. Pharisee.

Part B

1. The resurrection; angels; spirits.
2. They tempted, or tested, Him.

Part C.

2. Caiphas.
3. Ananias.
4. Nicodemus.

Resource 6

See answers in lesson 8, numbers 7, 8, 9, and 11.